peace after DIVORCE

*This book helped me to see specifically where I
was having problems that were preventing me
from moving on with my life. I can truly say that
my life, and who I am have been shaped by my
divorce, but it no longer defines me.*

Laura Hill

Renee Smith Ettline, M.Ed.

Jesse Press, LLC

PEACE AFTER DIVORCE

Published by Jesse Press, LLC, 1643B Savannah Hwy #180, Charleston, SC, 29407. Email: info@jessepress.com. Printed in the United States of America.

Source of unattributed scriptures and scriptures noted NIV:

Scripture taken from the *HOLY BIBLE, NEW INTERNATIONAL VERSION®.* Copyright © 1973, 1978, 1984 by International Bible Society. Used by permission of Zondervan Publishing House. All rights reserved.

The "NIV" and "New International Version" trademarks are registered in the United States Patent and Trademark Office by International Bible Society. Use of either trademark requires the permission of International Bible Society.

Other sources of noted scriptures are the following:

Scripture quotations marked NLT are taken from the *Holy Bible*, New Living Translation, copyright © 1996, 2004, 2007 by Tyndale House Foundation. Used by permission of Tyndale House Publishers, Inc., Carol Stream, Illinois 60188. All rights reserved.

Scripture taken from *THE MESSAGE*. Copyright© 1993, 1994, 1995, 1996, 2000, 2001, 2002. Used by permission of NavPress Publishing Group.

Scripture taken from the New King James Version. Copyright ©1979, 1980, 1982 by Thomas Nelson, Inc. Used by permission. All rights reserved.

Source of unattributed quotations: Renee Smith Ettline.

ISBN 978-0-9848789-9-4

Edited by Lisa Dodd
Cover Design by Eugean Taylor, artisancs@gmail.com
Photo of Authors by Karen Bloomer

Book order information is available at www.afterdivorceministries.com.

Acknowledgements

Only through God's greatness could the heartbreak of divorce transform into a meaningful ministry. I offer my endless gratitude for the love of Christ and the guidance of the Holy Spirit. The development of this book and the mission of helping those who hurt from divorce would be lifeless without it.

The support and insights of my husband Fred Ettline have been priceless. He has served as editor, contributor, and sounding board as well as dedicated spouse throughout the development of this book. My partner in ministry, and fellow veteran of divorce, he is a gift from God.

Several *After Divorce Ministries* team members have served as book reviewers. They are Jean Henderson, Elizabeth Holt, Tim Russell, Yvonne Smith, and Glenn Sutherland. My thanks and love to these Christians who have volunteered so much to support others on their journey to peace after divorce.

A special thanks to Roberta Grace who contributed her *Steps to Total Forgiveness*. I am also grateful to Lisa Dodd who has supported this book with her editing skills and to Lana Beckley who has helped me keep the faith through challenging times. Thank you also to the participants of our workshops from whom I have learned much.

Heartfelt thanks to Pastors Ron Hamilton and Chuck Sumner of Seacoast Church West Campus for their friendship, prayers, guidance, and leadership. Thanks to Pastor Greg Surratt, Senior Pastor, and all of the teaching pastors of Seacoast Church whose messages challenge us to find and take the mountain God has for us. Their inspiration is significant.

My parents Joe and Edith Smith taught me to love God and trust in Christ. The Christian values they instilled still strengthen and guide me today. For that, I am most grateful.

Renee Ettline

About the Book

Disclaimer--Use of This Publication Assumes the Following Understanding:

This publication provides information for personal reflection and evaluation. Content reflects insight of the author derived from education, divorce, and experience leading workshops for those divorced and divorcing, as well as the resources indicated. It is not designed to serve in lieu of counseling, psychological therapy, pastoral care, or other professional services. Seek professional services when needed. Neither author nor publisher shall have any responsibility or liability with respect to damage or loss caused by or allegedly caused by the contents of this book.

Examples in the text represent real stories. In most cases, fictitious first names are used to protect individual privacy. Actual identities are represented by first and last names and are used with permission.

This publication does not advocate divorce. However, divorce is a reality in our society. This book intends to help those whose lives are touched by its unsettling effects.

 **Renee Ettline** is founder of After Divorce Ministries, LLC, and creator of the Peace after Divorce Workshop Study. For information, visit www.afterdivorceministries.com. For answers to questions about offering the *Peace After Divorce* workshop series, you may email info@afterdivorceministries.com.

Table of Contents

Preface

A Message from Renee and Fred Ettline

Congratulations on your efforts to make your life better after separation and divorce. We have been through a divorce in the past. We know the pain. We know that peace after divorce is possible.

We are both Christians and educators who feel a calling to help others move beyond the sadness of divorce, just as God has helped us. This book is the result of a need we discovered as we started to develop our ministry. We wanted a book that would offer guidance, not just for getting through the immediacy of divorce, but also for moving beyond divorce. The book had to share real-life strategies as well as the power of God's love. When we did not find the book we wanted, Renee wrote *Peace after Divorce*.

Renee is a former counselor who worked with adults and students in college, industry, and school settings. Most of her career has involved teaching life strategies and skills. While she is not a psychologist or clergy, she draws on her background as well as her faith in the writing of this book. Fred is a retired college professor. As the custodial parent of two girls, his experiences were particularly helpful with the section of this book on helping children cope with divorce.

Each reading in the book will conclude with questions designed to help you apply section concepts to your life. Reflect on and pray about what you've read and then answer the questions.

Be patient with yourself. Realize that moving beyond the lingering impact of divorce will likely take more time than it takes to read this book. After finishing the book, keep it as a reference and revisit it as needed.

If You Are Reading on Your Own

Work through the book at a comfortable pace. Dashing through the chapters will likely put you on overload. Read no more than one chapter per week.

You absolutely can benefit from working through this book alone but if you would like expanded support, join a Peace after Divorce Workshop. If there is not one near you, you may wish to join the online self-study course at www.PeaceafterDivorceWorkshop.com.

If You Are Attending a Workshop

Attending an in-person *Peace after Divorce* Workshop gives you a great opportunity to learn with others who can relate to what you're going through. Groups are generally at churches and meet for eight to nine sessions.

Workshops are centered on the content of this book and are intended to offer participants the following:

- *A Non-Judgmental Environment*—You become a valued part in the group dynamics of the workshop. Share and learn from others who are addressing similar concerns.
- *Information*—Learn about adjustments and life choices related to finding peace after divorce.
- *Personalization*—Questions and group discussions allow you to personalize your progress toward finding peace after divorce.

- *Spiritual Support*—The workshop is Christ-centered. Reminders of the healing power, grace, love, and forgiveness of God permeate the ministry.

To benefit most, read the designated chapter between sessions, answer chapter questions, and attend each session.

Two Requirements for Workshop Participants

We ask that you not romance or date one another during the period of the workshop. Dating changes the workshop dynamic and diminishes each person's ability to focus on self-development. Additionally, workshop attendees are often still vulnerable and may find romantic advances during the weeks of the workshop to be uncomfortable.

Couples who are divorced, divorcing, or dating are not to attend this workshop together. While both members of a couple may benefit from this workshop, we require that you attend at different dates. Attending the workshop together would change the workshop dynamic and diminish each person's ability to focus on self-development.

Guidelines for Group Discussion
The following guidelines enhance group discussions and encourage peer support:

1. Remember, this is a structured ministry and peer-support group. It is not counseling or therapy.
2. You may say pass to any questions asked of you.
3. While you may discuss how this ministry affects you with whomever you choose, you are not free to repeat other's experiences or comments. By honoring confidentiality, you respect the privacy of all who are in your group and they in turn respect your privacy.*
4. Give each person a chance to speak.
5. Avoid side conversations.
6. Self-monitor to be sure you are not doing all the talking.
7. Keep discussion centered on the topics at hand.
8. Share ideas and experiences, but avoid directing others by saying things like "you shouldn't," or "you ought." It is not the purpose of this workshop to pass judgment.
9. Let kindness rule.

*PLEASE NOTE--If you reveal that you or anyone is in physical danger, workshop facilitators may share this with appropriate people in an effort to help prevent harm coming to you or others. No one involved with the workshop is covered legally by privileged conversation.

CHAPTER 1

TAKE CHARGE

> *The choice is yours—*
> *you do not have to be*
> *defined by your divorce.*

Are you feeling bent out of shape by divorce? You do not have to stay that way. With courage and determination, you have the power to influence the outcomes of your life in positive ways. The choice is yours—you do not have to be defined by your divorce.

The Threshold

'For I know the plans I have for you,'
declares the Lord, 'plans to prosper you
and not to harm you, plans to give you
hope and a future. Then you will call upon
me and come and pray to me, and I will
listen to you. You will seek me and find me
when you seek me with all your heart.'

Jeremiah 29:11-13 NIV

Devastated by the reality that divorce was inevitable, I crumbled inside. Sound thinking out the window and faith frazzled to a thread, I impulsively headed to the door. For a moment, the only answer seemed to be a deadly plunge from the highest span of a bridge.

As I opened the door and stepped over the threshold, logic broke through with an unexpected clarity. There had to be a better solution. Life was too valuable to toss away or muddle through because of a collision course with divorce. I decided to work through healing and to find a better life. It would not be easy, but it would be worth it.

The ability to renew life after divorce hinges on this threshold decision. You too must recognize your power to influence your life for the better, and you too must commit to doing just that. Your life is too valuable to settle for anything less. You have the power to step over the threshold now and begin the work of renewing your life after divorce.

2

Step by Step

That you are not powerless is probably the most important concept to wrap your brain around as you deal with divorce. You can't control all circumstances, but you can work within your reality to make your life better. You can exercise the power of choice to move in a positive direction. Furthermore, you can draw on the healing power of God to support and guide you along the way.

Divinely Empowered

When you renew your spirit by yielding your life to God, you enhance your ability to take charge of your life and to recover from divorce. This may seem contradictory at first, but it really isn't. Choosing to seek God's guidance and to make prayerfully considered decisions in faith is divinely empowering. For this reason, each section in this book reflects on scriptures, provides questions for applying content, and encourages prayer.

The Bible is full of stories of people who take charge of their choices and find recovery in God. In Acts 14:8-10 Paul claims God's healing for a man who has never been able to walk his whole life. The man not only shows faith in God's power, but also chooses to risk trying to stand up and walk. He could say, "Stand on these feet? You must be kidding!" However, he believes enough to follow through on his faith with action. "...the man jumped up and began to walk." The man believes God can heal him and then makes the choice to act in accordance with that faith by risking standing on his own feet.

Your choices will determine the degree to which you do the following:

- Allow God to help you renew your life after divorce.
- Stand on your own feet as a single person.
- Walk through life in victory.

Your past does not have to dictate your future. You have the God-given power to make your life better and to heal from divorce. Whether your divorce is pending, or occurred many years ago, you have just made a step forward by deciding to address related issues head-on.

God will empower you to do the work of recovering from divorce. "I can do everything through Him who gives me strength," says Philippians 4:13. God provides the strength, but you must be willing to reflect on your situation and to take action.

Taking charge of your life with God's guidance can move you to a place where your divorce no longer has an unsettling emotional influence in your life. God has "plans to prosper you and not to harm you, plans to give you hope and a future." You will find it when you seek him "with all of your heart" (Jeremiah 29:11-13).

Making Information and Ideas Work

1. What does a life defined by divorce look like?

4

2. What does it mean to you to know you do not have to live a life defined by your divorce?

3. What do the words of Jeremiah 29:11-13 mean to you?

4. Write a statement of your commitment to healing from divorce.

Talk with God--Ponder this reading and share your thoughts with God. Listen so that the Holy Spirit might fill you with wisdom and peace. What concrete actions do you need to take based on what God is saying to you?

That you are not powerless is probably the most important concept for you to wrap your brain around. You can't control all circumstances, but you can work within your reality to make your life better.

Choosing to seek God's guidance and to make prayerfully considered decisions in faith is divinely empowering.

God, Divorce, and Me

The Lord is close to the brokenhearted and
saves those who are crushed in spirit.

Psalms 34:18 NIV

"How can I ask God to help me move past divorce?" says Connie. "I mean, wouldn't that be asking him to help me with something I know he does not approve of in the first place?"

Connie is not alone in her concern. Awareness of the seriousness of the wedding vows leaves many confused about where they stand with God. To add to the confusion, different churches teach different things about divorce. What's more, scriptures on divorce can mean one thing on face value but may be understood more fully in light of the whole word of God and the times and cultures in which they were written.

Is It Okay to Ask God to Help Me Heal from Divorce?

So, what is the answer to Connie's question? Is it all right to ask God to help you move past divorce even when you know God means for marriage to last a lifetime? Of course it is. "The Lord is close to the brokenhearted," and that includes those healing from divorce. That does not mean that we should take the decision to divorce lightly.

6

Will Divorce Keep Me Out of Heaven?

"I've been divorced three times," says Sandra. "I'm not sure God will still let me into heaven." Sandra need not worry--success in marriage is not the criteria for salvation. Marriage vows are indeed serious, but salvation has to do with accepting Christ and following him. John 3:16 tells us "... whoever believes in him (Christ) shall not perish but have eternal life."

Is God Angry with Me?

The Bible never says God hates divorced people. Instead it says, "'I hate divorce,' says the Lord God of Israel," (Malachi 2:16). Because God loves us, it makes sense that he would hate divorce. As anyone touched by divorce knows, the spin-off affects everyone in the home as well as other family and friends. Divorce crushes spirits. However, Psalms 34:18 tells us that the Lord "saves those who are crushed in spirit." This is not a picture of an angry God. Instead, it reflects a God who recognizes and feels for us in our pain.

Will God Forgive Me for the Mistakes I Made in My Marriage?

Yes. God will forgive you if you earnestly ask God for forgiveness and then seek to live a life that follows him. When you do, you will find that God's grace is amazing. God loves you and is enormously compassionate. You must still deal with the earthly consequences of your choices, but God will be with you on your journey to peace after divorce.

Hear what Jesus said in John 8:3-11 to the woman who had committed adultery:

> *The teachers of the law and the Pharisees brought in a woman caught in adultery. They made her stand before the group and said to Jesus, "Teacher, this woman was caught in the act of adultery. In the Law Moses commanded us to stone such women. Now what do you say?" They were using this question as a trap, in order to have a basis for accusing him. But Jesus bent down and started to write on the ground with his finger. When they kept on questioning him, he straightened up and said to them, "If any one of you is without sin, let him be the first to throw a stone at her." Again he stooped down and wrote on the ground. At this, those who heard began to go away one at a time, the older ones first, until only Jesus was left, with the woman still standing there. Jesus straightened up and asked her, "Woman, where are they? Has no one condemned you?" "No one, sir," she said. "Then neither do I condemn you," Jesus declared. "Go now and leave your life of sin."*

---

*If your marriage has ended,
focusing on your failure to meet God's ideal
for marriage denies the love of God as
expressed through the death
and resurrection of Christ.
Your marriage may have ended, but God's
covenant with you will not fail.
God's love for you prevails.*

8

How Do I Thrive and Find Peace as a Christian Who is Divorced?

Remind yourself of these principles:

- My identity is in Christ alone, not in being divorced.
- God desires wholeness for me.
- God will grant me guidance if I ask.
- God knows the truth of my heart and he wants to heal what is broken.
- If I earnestly ask for forgiveness for my part in the breakdown of the marriage, God will forgive me.
- God loves me and wants me to have a joyful and spirit-filled life.
- I don't have to be defined by my past. God offers me a new life.
- God has a plan for me.

Realizing that divorce does not take away your importance to God frees you to have a healing relationship with him. Not only can you come to terms with your divorce and take charge of your life, you can do it with God's guidance and love.

Making Information and Ideas Work

1. Re-read the section entitled, "How Do I Thrive and Find Peace as a Christian Who is Divorced?" Circle the principles you need to focus on the most.

2. Reflect on the items you circled and their importance to your situation. Write your thoughts.

Talk with God--Ponder this reading and share your thoughts with God. Listen so that the Holy Spirit might fill you with wisdom and peace. What concrete actions do you need to take based on what God is saying to you?

*...Be Joyful. Grow to maturity.
Encourage each other. Live in harmony and
peace. Then the God of love and peace
will be with you.*
2 Corinthians 13:11

Accepting Divorce as Reality

*Humble yourselves, therefore, under God's
mighty hand, that he may lift you up in due
time. Cast all your anxiety on him because
he cares for you.*

1 Peter 5:6-7 NIV

The 'D' Word

For some time I could hardly say the word 'divorce.'
Tears flowed as it formed in my brain. Speaking it made it
all too real--but real it was.

For some, choosing to separate and divorce reflects acceptance that the marriage is ending. They are simply saying
last rites over a marriage that, in their minds, has been dead
for some time. Others, dazed by a spouse's seemingly ab-
rupt departure or discovered unfaithfulness, must work
through the fog of shock to accept the reality of divorce.

Making the choice to move forward means being willing
to accept the new truths of your life. Only when you accept
the reality of what has happened, or is happening, can you
grasp what you need to do to move to a better place.

Accepting the Math of Marriage and Divorce

Marriage unites two people into one (Genesis 2:24). Because of this, it can be easy to feel less than whole when a
marriage ends. Feeling less than whole can make it harder to
accept divorce as your reality. You are not less than whole

11

when you divorce. Personal wholeness does not come from another human being. It comes only from a relationship with God. "Salvation is found in no one else, for there is no other name under heaven given to men by which we must be saved" (Acts 4:12).

Although it takes two people to make a marriage, it only takes one to end it. For marriage to thrive, two people must be willing to honor their marriage vows. Both husband and wife must believe the marriage is worth saving and be willing to do the work to save it. If one partner resolves that the marriage has ended, the marriage is no more.

The Reality of Free Will

"I've been through lots of counseling and done everything I know to do to save my marriage," said Anne. "I've asked God to make my husband change. He doesn't change. Things just get worse. I feel like a failure."

The marriage covenant is serious. Seeking God's guidance and working hard to save your marriage is appropriate, but so is an awareness of God's gift of free will. You cannot force your spouse to want to make your marriage work. Even God does not force people to act in certain ways. God stands at the door and knocks (Revelation 3:20).

A realistic look at how your spouse is exercising free will over time can help you to assess the reality of your situation. Otherwise, you may spend years trying to save a marriage with no success because you are the only one investing the needed energy. It is like trying to canoe with a paddle on only one side. There is a tendency to keep going in circles rather than moving forward.

12

Deliverance--The Other "D" Word

Uttering the word divorce without tears welling in my eyes came slowly. I was not happy about divorce, but came to accept its reality. Eventually, I could check divorced as my marital status on a form without cringing. Accepting the reality of divorce was a key step toward deliverance from its devastating grip.

If divorce is your reality, then accepting that reality opens the door to getting your life together. Supported by prayer and faith you can actively work through the issues of divorce and find peace and joy in God, as well as a positive sense of yourself. It takes effort, but the pay-off is well worth it. Cast your anxiety on God throughout the process and he will lift you up in due time (1 Peter 5:6-7 NIV).

Making Information and Ideas Work

1. Why does it only take one person to end a marriage?

2. What do you need to do to accept divorce as your reality?

3. How is accepting the reality of your divorce fundamental to finding peace after separation and divorce?

Talk with God--Ponder this reading and share your thoughts with God. Listen so that the Holy Spirit might fill you with wisdom and peace. What concrete actions do you need to take based on what God is saying to you?

You Mean I'm Normal?

Hearing other's experiences made me feel that I wasn't crazy, that I'm doing great for where I am right now.

After Divorce Ministries Workshop Participant

Divorce is a rollercoaster of conflicting emotions and changing circumstances. Many people report feeling that they are going crazy. Knowing your experiences are common can help you feel less crazy and more capable of taking responsibility for your own life.

Look over the items in the following chart. Check the box beside each statement that reflects a feeling, thought, or experience you have had since your separation or divorce. Move quickly over the list since your first instinct is probably right. Be honest.

Note: The phrase "former spouse" throughout this book refers to soon-to-be former spouses as well as former spouses.

Self-Assessment of Experiences

☒ I feel like I'm going crazy.

☐ I lost weight during my divorce. *Gained*

☒ I wish my former spouse would explain why.

☒ I'm fearful.

☒ I'm confused.

☒ My world isn't stable.

☐ I feel aimless.

☒ I feel very alone.

☒ I'm often wondering – could I have done more?

☒ I constantly think about my divorce.

☒ I wish I had…

☒ I cry a lot.

☒ I can't concentrate well.

☒ I'm a good person, so why didn't my marriage work?

☒ I'm sad a lot of the time.

☒ I feel guilty.

☐ I never knew I could be this angry.

☐ I'm stunned. I cannot believe this.

☐ I don't trust the opposite sex.

☐ I have a short fuse and am easily angered or irritated.

☒ I'm worried about finances.

☐ I feel guilty for having left.

☒ I'm struggling with changes in family relationships.

☐ I feel abused.

☒ Holidays make me bluer.

☒ My sleep patterns are messed up.

☒ I never thought I'd be divorced.

☐ I don't seem to have as much energy as before.

☒ I cannot believe this has happened.

☒ I feel rejected or devalued.

- ☐ I'm distressed - I've had more than one failed marriage.
- ☐ Is God mad at me?
- ☐ I wish someone understood what I'm going through.
- ☒ I am afraid I'll get back into the same type relationship.
- ☒ Our former friends do not come around anymore.
- ☒ My heart feels so much loss.
- ☒ It is over, but I can't let go.
- ☐ My eating patterns are messed up.
- ☒ I've been unhappy for a long time, so why do I feel guilty?
- ☒ My emotions are all over the place.
- ☒ I'd like to date, but I'm scared.
- ☐ I want to get back at my former spouse.
- ☐ Is it possible to be happy being single?
- ☒ I want to run away and hide.
- ☒ I'm worried about my kids and divorce.
- ☒ I need to know what to do to get back on my feet after divorce.

The Comfort of Normal

Not everyone experiences everything on the checklist because our situations and experiences are not exactly alike. However, if you checked anything on the list, you are experiencing a feeling or thought that we have observed to be common for someone directly impacted by the turbulence of divorce. We hope you will find this comforting and somewhat liberating as you strive to take charge of your life. Successfully and prayerfully working through the spin-off of your divorce will help you to move to a less crazy-feeling place.

Making Information and Ideas Work

1. To which three statements on the checklist do you most relate?

2. What does this say to you about things you need to work on as you deal with divorce?

3. What impact does it have on you to know your reactions to divorce are common?

Talk with God--Ponder this reading and share your thoughts with God. Listen so that the Holy Spirit might fill you with wisdom and peace. What concrete actions do you need to take based on what God is saying to you?

Navigating the Winds of Divorce

*I praise you because I am fearfully and
wonderfully made; your works are
wonderful, I know that full well.*

Psalm 139:14 NIV

Propelled by the wind, the sailboat cut through the water
and with amazing speed headed directly toward the port side
of another boat. With swift action, the crew skillfully
changed the rudder and sail. A collision was averted.
Changing the rudder and sail redirected their course despite
their inability to change the wind.

The threshold decision to take charge of your life prayerfully launches you on your journey to peace after divorce.
Much remains to be done and you must work through wind-
swept waters along the way. By adjusting your rudder and
sail as needed, you will eventually find your way to smoother waters. Taking responsibility for your own destiny makes
that possible and is within your reach because God's wonderful design has blessed you with the ability to better yourself by the choices you make.

When a Former Spouse is behind the Wind

An advantage of prayerfully taking responsibility for your
own course to peace after divorce is that you stop letting
your outcomes rest totally on the choices of your former
spouse. Dwelling on your former spouse's responsibility for

18

situations leaves you tossed about by the wind. For example, if you believe your happiness is dependent on how your former spouse is behaving, you set yourself up to be disappointed. If you believe your life can only be better if your former spouse changes, you have set yourself up for a downward spiral of frustration. You cannot change the choices your former spouse makes. However, you can make choices to redirect the course of your own life.

Navigating Your Way

Body, mind, and spirit are affected by the winds of divorce. What you feel, think, believe, and the actions you choose, all come into play when charting a course for moving on with your life. Navigating your way to a positive life after divorce requires taking a good look at where you are and what you need to change to get where you want to go. It means allowing God to serve as your lighthouse along the way. It also requires recognizing that while you may have to live with circumstances created by your ex, you do not have to be a victim tossed about at sea.

A feeling of control is central to being able to overcome adversity. Ask yourself these three questions:

1. What is in my power to change so that I will have better outcomes?

2. How can I get the most out of the resources I have?

3. Am I keeping my eye on the lighthouse of God as I work through the turbulent waters that have resulted from my divorce?

You may have to ask these questions several times a day as you navigate your course. Knowing the answers to these questions as it relates to various challenges will help you to find more control and peace in your life.

Jesus the Lighthouse

"Lord it is you," Peter replied, "tell me to come to you on the water."

"Come," he said. Then Peter got down out of the boat, walked on the water and came toward Jesus. But when he saw the wind, he was afraid and beginning to sink, cried out, "Lord, save me!"

Immediately Jesus reached out his hand and caught him. "You of little faith," he said, "why did you doubt?" And then they climbed into the boat and the wind died down.

Matthew 14:28-32

Making Information and Ideas Work

1. In what ways do you feel tossed about by divorce?

2. How can taking responsibility for yourself reduce your former spouse's control in your life?

3. Given your resources, what one thing can you change this week to help you have a better outcome as you navigate the winds of divorce?

Talk with God--Ponder this reading and share your thoughts with God. Listen so that the Holy Spirit might fill you with wisdom and peace. What concrete actions do you need to take based on what God is saying to you?

Highlights from Chapter 1--Take Charge

1. Committing to do the work needed to heal from divorce is a threshold decision.

2. Your past does not have to dictate your future because God has blessed you with the ability to better yourself by the choices you make.

3. God knows divorce hurts. He has compassion for you.

4. God offers forgiveness for our mistakes if we change our ways and earnestly follow Him.

5. Moving past divorce includes prayerfully accepting responsibility for yourself.

6. Taking charge of yourself empowers you rather than leaving you living like a victim.

7. It only takes one person committed to ending the marriage for it to end.

8. You cannot force your spouse to do anything.

9. If divorce is your reality, then accepting that reality opens the door to getting your life together.

10. You can find peace, joy, and a positive new life by proactively working through the issues of divorce.

11. God has a plan for your future and wants you to have a joyful, spirit-filled life.

CHAPTER 2

SEEK RENEWAL

*Working with God through divorce
is like dancing with God leading.
The dance is much smoother if you pick up
your feet and follow.*

Divorce redesigns the world as you have come to know it. Changes to daily life may overwhelm and rattle you at first. Tackling these changes by developing resources and learning to make well-informed choices can give you a greater sense of control as well as better outcomes. Learning to manage the changes can also allow you to put more energy into your overall renewal from divorce.

Seeking renewal for your life after divorce is a choice you make. Choosing to accept God's help and guidance includes being willing to pick up your feet and follow. Renewal requires faith and action as you face the changes in your life head-on.

Moving from Acceptance to Renewal

*He waited seven more days and again sent
out the dove from the ark. When the dove returned
to him in the evening, there in its beak was a freshly
plucked olive leaf! Then Noah knew that the water
had receded from the earth.*

Genesis 8:10-11 NIV

Noah had lived through the flood. The waters were receding and he now had the hope of a new beginning. You too have the hope of a new beginning as you work through the issues of your divorce and look to the future. With faith and work, you can successfully mend the wounds of divorce; redefine yourself as a single person; and move forward to a place of peace, joy, and fulfillment.

Gaining insight into the impact of divorce can help you to understand yourself better. Prayerfully working through relevant questions can help you make personal moves toward renewal. Implementing strategies for renewing your life can help you continue to progress toward a healthier and more fulfilled existence. Combine all of this with knowing that God loves you and has a plan for your life, and the results can be amazing. After all, God can "do immeasurably more than all we ask or imagine, according to his power that is at work within us," (Ephesians 3:20).

How Long Will it Take?

Time heals all wounds--or does it? Not really. The mere passage of time does not heal hurts. Becoming renewed after divorce is a gradual growth process. No one can predict with certainty how long each individual's healing and renewal will take.

What Contributes to Finding Renewal and Peace after Divorce?

Recovering from separation and divorce is a decision, a process, and a journey of faith. The exact process and specific goals along the way depend on your unique situation. Finding renewal after divorce entails making choices to adapt positively to the realities of your divorce, finding empowerment to heal, and actively pursuing a positive new direction. This means making decisions to work through your divorce until it no longer pushes your buttons.

No Magic Formula

Because renewal after divorce is a personal journey, it is impossible to come up with a one-size-fits-all formula. However, some components of the journey are common. Exploring these and determining how they relate to you can help you move forward.

God designed you to be unique. Accordingly, your renewal after divorce will depend on the blend of your unique situation, experiences, and focused effort. Set your sites on renewal, but be patient with yourself.

Making Information and Ideas Work

1. What does it mean to you to recover from divorce?

2. A timeline of emotionally significant events in your marriage provides a good point of reference for some of the work you will do as you renew your life after separation and divorce. The example on the next page shows some of the types of things that might appear on a timeline of personally significant events. Read over the example in preparation for completing your own timeline.

3. Reviewing the significant emotional events of your marriage may help you gain a more realistic perspective and may reveal patterns as well. Think through your relationship with your former spouse from the day you met until now. Create your own timeline on page 28 or on a sheet of paper. Write down the events that represent memories that have the most negative or most positive emotional impact. Keep the lists in overall chronological order. Keep your timeline in a private place and add to it as things come to mind.

Sample Timeline
Significant Memories about My Ex

Starting with the Day We Met	
Memories with Positive Impact:	**Memories with Negative Impact:**
We met	
You sent me roses	
	You lied to me
We got engaged	
We got married	
You got a promotion	
We moved to Florida	
We bought our first house	
	You really put me down at dinner at friend's house
Our child was born	
We went to Colorado for vacation	You stopped helping me
You encouraged me to return to school	
We moved back to our home state	
	Your debt soared
I got a new job and new friends	
	You lost your job
	You would disappear
	You dropped out of marriage counseling
	I moved out while you were away to avoid conflict
	Our custody battle
	Our divorce
	I saw you with another
Ending with Today	

27

Personal Timeline
Significant Memories about My Ex

Starting with the Day We Met

Memories with Positive Impact:	Memories with Negative Impact:

Ending with Today

A Foundation for Discovery

Completing your timeline may have been both an emotional and a revealing process. Reflecting on it may help you begin to get a grip on the overall experience of your marriage relationship. You may see patterns you have not noticed before. Have the bad times outweighed the good for some time now? Does it reveal repeated patterns in your spouse's behavior? Perhaps your timeline reveals sources of anger and unforgiveness, or patterns of refusing to let go. Don't hesitate to add other things as they come to mind since the timeline is a foundation for other activities in this book.

Visit the Past to Find the Future

Reflecting on the past and committing to move forward with your life can be scary, but it can also be exciting. As the flood waters of divorce begin to recede, you will start to see glimpses of your new beginning. Anxieties about bringing closure to the past and establishing a new life can be replaced with confidence when you remember the promise of Jeremiah 29:11-13. It reminds you that God has a plan for you--a plan for a future and a hope.

Talk with God--Ponder this reading and share your thoughts with God. Listen so that the Holy Spirit might fill you with wisdom and peace. What concrete actions do you need to take based on what God is saying to you?

Embracing a World of Change

*In the beginning God created the heavens and
the earth. Now the earth was formless and empty,
darkness was over the surface of the deep,
and the Spirit of God was hovering over the waters.*

Genesis 1:1-2 NIV

A New Cup

I handed my paper cup to the young man at the fast food
restaurant and requested a refill. The manager observed and
directed the young man to give me a new cup. "She don't
want no new cup," asserted the young man quite seriously
as I stood silently. "People get attached to their cups," he
added. "Don't go off on me," said the manager. Under pro-
test, the young man got a new cup mumbling all the while,
"People get attached to their cup, man. People don't want no
new cup."

It was just a paper cup. But sometimes even simple
changes can throw people off balance, especially when
those changes are not anticipated. If even small changes can
rattle our comfort zone, it is no wonder that the vast changes
of divorce can rock our worlds.

The Turmoil of Divorce

Change is the order of the day with divorce. Basic things
like housing and financial issues must be resolved. Relation-

ships with friends and family may change. Uncertainties exist about whom to trust. Plans for the future must be rethought. The well-being of children is a concern. To compound things, all this must be processed with a brain that is likely flooded with conflicting emotions. It is common to feel rather numb.

Taking on Change

At first just keeping your head above water may feel like a challenge. One moment at a time, you can begin to adapt to your new life, let go of the past, and start to embrace the changes of your life. Embracing change means letting go of your former spouse and letting go of the past. It means trying to figure out what you can learn from your current challenges and experiences. It means becoming independent and prayerfully self-directed.

Developing Resources

Becoming independent of your spouse means assuming responsibility for things your spouse has been handling. Developing a support network can help to see you through this logistical and emotional transition. I'm not a mechanic so developing a working relationship with someone in an automotive repair shop gave me a valuable resource when I divorced. Positive friendships with people who had experienced divorce and moved on with their lives gave me a different type of resource.

Having people you can rely on can help reduce the sense of turmoil associated with divorce. Identify the areas in which you need help and seek out needed resources. Keep in mind that developing a strong support network is not the same as failing to be responsible for yourself.

Turning Turmoil into Something Good

One of the greatest resources you can have is a relationship with God. If your divorce leaves your world feeling formless, empty and dark, know that God is hovering over your troubled waters. Creating fine things out of disorder is God's specialty. Partnering with God as you recover from divorce entails faith. Faith is a choice you make to believe that God will help you to heal and to find a better life.

Embracing a Mindset of Faith

When faith becomes your mindset, you realize that you can have hope. Hope makes it easier to look for positive change. The choice to have a mindset of faith can help you to gain a positive new perspective on yourself. A mindset of faith also can help you to identify a positive new direction in your life, and to seek positive new experiences one day at a time.

Taking Action

Cultivating positive change in your life is like growing a garden. It takes the power of God's creation and the efforts of the gardener. You must become an active gardener if you expect yourself to grow. Work through each section in this book and set your mind on prayerfully creating positive change in your life.

Making Information and Ideas Work

1. What changes related to your divorce have created the most turmoil in your life?

2. What impact has divorce had on your relationships with friends and family?

3. What resources do you have to help you with changes related to divorce?

4. How can the choice to have a mindset of faith lead you in a more positive direction?

5. How is your mindset affecting your ability to heal from divorce?

Talk with God--Ponder this reading and share your thoughts with God. Listen so that the Holy Spirit might fill you with wisdom and peace. What concrete actions do you need to take based on what God is saying to you?

Making Choices about Change

*God, give us grace to accept with serenity the things
that cannot be changed, Courage to change the things
which should be changed, and the Wisdom
to distinguish the one from the other.
Living one day at a time, enjoying one moment at a time,
accepting hardship as a pathway to peace, taking as
Jesus did, this sinful world as it is, not as I would have it,
trusting that You will make all things right, if I surrender
to Your will, so that I may be reasonably happy in this
life, and supremely happy with You forever in the next.*

Reinhold Niebuhr (1892-1971)[1]

One of the biggest challenges in dealing with the adjustments that come from divorce is deciding which things are within your control and which things are not. Making that distinction allows for letting go of things you can do nothing about, thus freeing you to apply your energies to those areas where you can make things better. It makes your efforts more productive while at the same time making you less frustrated. The original *Serenity Prayer,* by Reinhold Niebuhr, and its updated versions have likely become popular because it focuses clearly on this idea.

The Things That Cannot Be Changed

Trying to change things over which you have no control is as productive as leaning on a skyscraper trying to move it over a foot. All you get for your effort is tired and weary. At times, the only sane thing to do is accept things as they are, because no matter how hard you try, you cannot change them. Accepting this may require concentrated effort given the emotional nature of divorce.

Dealing with Situations You Can Change

In times of turmoil, it may be particularly difficult to feel like you can take charge of anything. Taking charge even in a small way is empowering and can make you feel less overwhelmed. It can give you a sense of success as you experience a positive outcome from your actions.

Taking charge of little things can move you forward one small step at a time. One woman stated that as she approached her divorce, the only thing she felt like she could keep organized in her life was her nightstand. It made her feel better to take control of that space. There may be times during divorce when life seems that overwhelming. If so, follow her example and find at least one little area you can keep in order until the seas become calm enough for you to move forward to bigger goals.

Ineffective Strategies for Dealing with Changes Associated with Divorce

What follows are some of the ineffective strategies we have seen people use to deal with the changes of divorce. Each of these strategies may stall or even derail finding peace after divorce. Don't feel bad if you see yourself dealing in some of these ways. Just ask God what you can learn from the revelation. Next, change the things you need to change in order to move your life to a better place. As you read about these less than productive ways to deal with the changes of divorce, circle approaches you've been using.

The Icicle Approach

I know there are things I should work on changing, but I just freeze up. I'm overwhelmed. Feeling numb in the early stages of a trauma may be common and can even serve a purpose. Staying in that frame of mind for an extended time is counterproductive.

The Rearview Mirror Approach

I have trouble moving forward because I am always looking back, holding on to what was, and what might have been. The rearview mirror has value if used to learn from the past, but if you drive a car looking into the rearview mirror most of the time, you'll have trouble getting where you are going.

The Daydreaming Approach

I daydream about how life might be but never take steps to make my dreams come true. Daydreaming is good if it motivates you to act to achieve those dreams. A lack of action will just leave you with empty dreams.

The Bulldozer Approach

I tend to make impulsive decisions with little forethought or consideration of the consequences. Anger and frustration are likely at the root of this approach. Your anger may be justified, but it can disrupt your life if you give it power.

The Avoidance Approach

If I don't deal with it, it cannot be happening. You may spend longer hours at work, stay overly busy with activities, sleep too much, or avoid reality by using alcohol or drugs. Perhaps you avoid what is happening by procrastinating and not taking actions you know you need to take. This approach offers no good future. Avoiding facing your reality will not move you forward.

The Blame Approach

What I'm dealing with is not my fault. Concentrating on placing blame allows you to avoid taking responsibility for what you can do to make your life better. With the blame approach, you give away your power to the person you blame.

The Flight Approach

I'll make any change that will remove me physically or psychologically as much as possible from my current situa-

tion even though those decisions may not be rational. The problem with this approach is that you can never run far enough if the problems are within you. Dealing head-on with a problem is generally the best way to work through it.

The Wallowing Approach
I've been done wrong and I'm gonna soak in it. Life stinks. Things always go wrong anyway so why try to make life better? Feeling bummed about divorce is natural, but settling into this doom and gloom mentality takes you lower and lower.

The Isolation Approach
I'm doing my best to isolate myself from everyone and everything. I'm afraid of change so I'll just lie low. This approach is a recipe for a stagnant life lived short of its potential.

Make Changes Work for You
Changes related to life after divorce come in a variety of forms. Changes may be what you want or may be the consequence of someone else's choices. Either way, you get to choose how you deal with them.

The first step in making changes work for you is to recognize when you are stuck in a less than productive way of dealing with change. The second step is to stop doing whatever is getting you stuck. The third step is to acknowledge that the powerful emotions of divorce can hinder your making the best decisions. The fourth step is to do what is rational rather than what feels right at the moment. Seek

Healing is a decision,
a process & a journey
of faith.

God's guidance and be intentional about making positive choices.

✕ Ten Questions for Making Rational Changes ✕

When considering an area where you need change, first make sure that the change you are considering is in fact achievable. Then explore answers to these ten questions:

1. What are the risks associated with this change?
2. What are the benefits associated with this change?
3. What information will help me make the best change?
4. What different paths might I take to make this change happen positively?
5. What are the good and bad things about each of these alternatives?
6. What barriers might I run into with each of the possible alternatives?
7. How can I deal with each of these barriers?
8. Which of the alternatives will best help achieve a positive change?
9. What steps must I take to implement the change?
10. How long will it take to make this change?

After evaluating the answers to these questions, you can make a plan for change and begin to implement it making any adjustments needed along the way. Exploring answers to these questions can help you to figure out why you are reluctant to make a given change. It can also help you to identify the risks and benefits of a potential change and to choose the best way to make a change.

Making Information and Ideas Work

1. Read the two examples that follow and then make your own list of issues related to your divorce that you cannot change, but that you are having trouble accepting.

   Example 1: My former spouse should want to see our children more.

   Example 2: My spouse should never have cheated on me.

2. For each issue you wrote to complete number 1, write a rational statement that reminds you that the issue is something you cannot change, and therefore is something upon which you must stop dwelling. After you write a statement, read it aloud and ask God if the statement represents the wisdom you need to help yourself let go of the issue you have identified. Rewrite the statement if you need. Repeat that statement to yourself whenever you find yourself getting frustrated.

   Example 1: That may be true, but I have no control over him (or her.) I must let go.

Example 2: True, but it is real. I cannot change it. I must let go and move on.

3. Describe two changes, within your control, that you need to make to help you move forward from divorce.

   Example 1: I can control my thoughts and my decisions.

   Example 2: I can stop calling my former spouse.

4. Reflect on the changes you identified in number 3 and think about them in light of *Ten Questions for Making Rational Changes* found in this section.

Talk with God--Ponder this reading and share your thoughts with God. Listen so that the Holy Spirit might fill you with wisdom and peace. What concrete actions do you need to take based on what God is saying to you?

Missed the Best of Life?

If God gives such attention to the appearance of wild-flowers—most of which are never even seen—don't you think he'll attend to you, take pride in you, do his best for you? What I'm trying to do here is to get you to re-lax, to not be so preoccupied with getting, so you can respond to God's giving. People who don't know God and the way he works fuss over these things, but you know both God and how he works. Steep your life in God-reality, God-initiative, God-provisions. Don't worry about missing out. You'll find all your everyday human concerns will be met.

Matthew 6:31-33 THE MESSAGE

The losses of divorce can be very jarring and may result in a sense of missing the best in life. That feeling is not from God. You can tell it is not from God by the lack of peace it brings to you. God brings us hope, peace, and renewal. Prayerfully working through loss is an important part of seeking renewal after divorce.

Thinking you have missed the best of life holds you back. It keeps you from being open to all God has in mind for you. It shuts your mind to his endless possibilities. When you start thinking you've missed the best in life, say, "I will no longer limit myself and God's ability to work in my life by believing I've missed the best in life."

Hope in Times of Trouble

God does not promise us a life free of trouble. In fact, the Bible clearly tells us we will have trouble in this world. Granted, that part is evident. The Bible also tells us that Jesus has overcome the world (John 16:33).

No one who is suffering is likely to get very excited about being told to rejoice in suffering. But Romans 5:1-5 is not telling us to be glad that we are suffering, it is telling us that we are to rejoice because we can know that if we persevere, God will help us to grow through our suffering. Persevering through our troubles builds our characters, which leads us to hope. Hope comes from choosing to trust God. Hope says that despite our losses, we can know that what God offers to our future is better than anything we may have missed in life. We just have to latch on to that truth.

Perseverance

Therefore, since we have been justified through faith, we have peace with God through our Lord Jesus Christ, through whom we have gained access by faith into this grace in which we now stand. And we rejoice in the hope of the glory of God. Not only so, but we also rejoice in our sufferings, because we know that suffering produces perseverance; perseverance, character; and character, hope. And hope does not disappoint us, because God has poured out his love into our hearts by the Holy Spirit, whom he has given us.

Romans 5:1-5 NIV

Renewing your life after divorce is a process. It takes time, but that does not mean the best in your life is over. Have a spirit that looks wholeheartedly for what God has planned for you. As the scripture states, "Steep your life in God-reality, God-initiative, God-provisions. Don't worry about missing out. You'll find all your everyday human concerns will be met" (Matthew 6:31-33, The Message).

Refuse to live a life flattened by disappointment. Jesus died for you. That's a lot of love and compassion for your well-being. Stir a passion deep inside and be determined to have the awesome spiritual life Jesus died to give you.

Making Information and Ideas Work

1. How do you see yourself growing in perseverance and character?

2. How does knowing that Jesus promises you a better life make you feel?

3. Write a statement claiming that you will have the best Jesus died to give you.

Talk with God--Ponder this reading and share your thoughts with God. Listen so that the Holy Spirit might fill you with wisdom and peace. What concrete actions do you need to take based on what God is saying to you?

Managing Daily Life

Hear my cry, O God; listen to my prayer.
From the ends of the earth I call to you,
I call as my heart grows faint; lead me to the rock that is
higher than I. For you have been my refuge, a strong tow-
er against the foe. I long to dwell in your tent forever and
take refuge in the shelter of your wings.

Psalm 61:1-4 NIV

Life as a newly single person can seem overwhelming. Initially just keeping your head above water can take most of your energy. Your resources diminish and your responsibilities increase as you take over the tasks previously handled by your former spouse.

Assessing responsibilities, priorities, and finances can jump-start you on your way to managing the realities of your new life. Once you have a solid grasp of where you are in each of these areas, you can develop techniques to help yourself cope. Increasing your control is one way to diminish your stress level and support your renewal.

Start With the Big Picture

Make a list of your responsibilities as a single person. Use basic tools such as keeping a calendar of upcoming commitments. Getting organized helps you to stay sane while doing tasks you've always done as well as assuming responsibility for the tasks your former spouse did.

Make a To-Do List of Tasks for Each Day

Assess how much time you need to allot for each task. Don't set yourself up for failure by planning to complete more tasks in a day than is humanly possible. On the other hand, do take charge of your day and make things happen rather than always putting things off until tomorrow.

Set Daily Priorities

With added responsibilities, your priorities may need to shift. Some tasks that in the past have seemed essential may be optional in your changed circumstances. Other responsibilities may need to be simplified, for example, minimizing the amount of yard work that needs to be done. Understand the differences among what is important, what is urgent, and what is optional. Doing the most urgent and most unpleasant tasks first to get them over can decrease your stress level.

Assess Your Finances and Develop a Budget

Finances are often a source of stress. If finances are tight, making ends meet may be a concern. Even if finances are not scarce, learning to manage those resources as a single person may be intimidating.

Take charge of your finances. Luke 14:28-30 says, "Suppose one of you wants to build a tower. Will he not first sit down and estimate the cost to see if he has enough money to complete it? For if he lays the foundation and is not able to finish it, everyone who sees it will ridicule him, saying, 'This fellow began to build and was not able to finish.'" This passage from Luke highlights the importance of financial planning, budgeting, and living within your means.

Analyze your expenses and your income. In what ways does your lifestyle need to change? Develop a budget to help you manage your cash flow. If debt is an issue, develop a plan for becoming debt free. Set financial goals then identify and implement a plan for meeting them.

Take Time to Pray and Study God's Word

As crazy as it sounds to add one more thing to your list of things to do, talking with God can help ease your burden so that you may approach your day with a greater sense of calm. Calm helps you manage much more efficiently than does a state of anxiety.

Making Information and Ideas Work

1. Make a list of the responsibilities that have been added to your plate since your separation or divorce.

2. Are any of your responsibilities things that could be scaled down or eliminated? How?

3. Use a calendar to record upcoming commitments.

4. Write a to-do list of tasks you need to accomplish on each day of the coming week.

5. Set priorities. Review your to-do-list from number 4 and rate each item in terms of priority.

6. Review your finances and develop a budget.

7. Name two things you can do to re-structure your life so that you have more time to relate to God.

Talk with God--Ponder this reading and share your thoughts with God. Listen so that the Holy Spirit might fill you with wisdom and peace. What concrete actions do you need to take based on what God is saying to you?

Opening a Direct Line to God

And pray in the Spirit on all occasions with all kinds of prayers and requests. With this in mind, be alert and always keep on praying for all the Lord's people.

Ephesians 6:18 NIV

Prayer gives you a direct link to the greatest resource available. After all, God specializes in renewal. In times of trouble as well as times of joy, prayer is a line straight to God. So why do so many people talk so little with God? Perhaps they have wrong-headed ideas about prayer. Perhaps they just don't know the value of prayer or the truth about God.

The value of prayer is that it is amazingly powerful in so many ways. The truth about God is that the relationship he seeks with you is personal. He created you so he knows you and loves you with an incredible love. God is great and almighty, but he is also approachable and is with you one-hundred percent of the time. Prayer allows you to tap into his presence.

How Do You Talk with God?

Talk with God simply, sincerely, and respectfully. You don't need fancy words. Realize that nobody, including you, can be good enough to merit God's love, but he gives it to you anyway. Clear the air by asking God for forgiveness and by forgiving those who have offended you. Thank God for his goodness and for loving you. Acknowledge God as being God. Pray in a way that is consistent with the teachings and Spirit of God. Don't ask for things that you know in your heart are wrong or incompatible with a follower of Christ.

Pray believing these things:
- God cares about you and your trials.
- God is with you.
- God loves you.
- God wants what is best for you.
- God knows best and knows the big picture. Ask that his will be done.
- God listens.
- Prayer can affect outcomes.

When You Don't Know What to Pray

Even if you don't know what to say to God, you can still pray. God already knows your heart. If words just won't come, quiet yourself and simply say, God, here I am. You know my heart.

"In the same way, the Spirit helps us in our weakness. We do not know what we ought to pray for, but the Spirit himself intercedes for us with groans that words cannot express. And he who searches our hearts knows the mind of the Spirit, because the Spirit intercedes for the saints in accordance with God's will." Romans 8:26-27

Pray God's Promises

Since the Bible tells God's promises, praying them just makes sense. Here are some examples of praying promises in the scriptures:

- Pray Jeremiah 29:11-14. Lord, thank you for having plans to give me a future and a hope. Thank you that you listen to me when I call upon you and pray to you. Thank you that I will find you when I seek you with all of my heart.

- Pray Psalms 34:18. Lord, thank you that you are close to the broken-hearted and that you save those who are crushed in spirit.

- Pray John 16:33. Lord, I know that even though I have troubles, you have overcome the world. Help me to take heart and to have peace.

Try Streaming Prayer

A running conversation with God is a great way to develop your relationship with him. Prayer does not have to be formal. Talk with God throughout the day. In the Bible, Paul says, "Be joyful always; pray continually; give thanks in all circumstances, for this is God's will for you in Christ Jesus." 1 Thessalonians 5:16-18.

Unanswered Prayer

When prayers seem to be unanswered, it can be hard to understand. Perhaps it is because the prayer was not in line with God's will. 1 John 5:14-15 tells us, "This is the confidence we have in approaching God: that if we ask anything according to his will, he hears us. And if we know that he hears us—whatever we ask—we know that we have what we asked of him."

God may not answer a prayer if it asks God to override the gift of free will that he has given to people. Praying on behalf of another person or asking for God's will to be done in someone's life is different from asking God to force another person act a certain way. Prayers may also seem unanswered because answers to prayers may not come quickly. 1 Peter 5:6 says, "Humble yourselves, therefore, under God's mighty hand, that he may lift you up in due time." God's timing can require waiting on God.

The truth is that God has the big picture and we do not. We don't understand about answers to our prayers because we can't conceive the mind of God. 1 Corinthians 2:7 says, "No, we speak of God's secret wisdom, a wisdom that has been hidden and that God destined for our glory before time began." Even when we don't understand, we can trust that God's wisdom exceeds ours and is in our best interest. That is why it is important to pray that God's will be done.

24/7 with God

Opening a dialog with God as you seek to renew your life after divorce has many advantages. God's vision and ability is unlimited. His strength and guidance are yours for the asking. His door is open 24-hours a day, seven days a week. You never have to leave God a voice mail. He is all powerful. He loves you. Furthermore, praying to God is amazingly easy.

6 Prayer Tips
From *After Divorce Ministries*
Workshop Participants

- Write Letters to God--Doing so helps focus your prayer needs. It reminds you that God is a friend.

- Have a God Space–Identify a quiet place where you can slow the pace and feel close to God every day.

- Thank God throughout the Day--It helps to keep you focused on the positive.

- Have a Peace Box—Write notes as prayer needs come to mind and put them in the box. Pull them out and talk to God about them daily.

- Build a "Good Day" List--Write a gratitude list on good days and read it to lift your spirit on bad days.

- Create Sticky Notes from God—Write encouraging scriptures on sticky notes and post them in your house and car. Read them as you see them and thank God for his word.

Making Information and Ideas Work

1. What role is prayer playing in your renewal?

2. Write in your own words the most meaningful thing you learned about prayer from this reading.

3. How can you benefit from your knowledge of the power of prayer and the truth about God?

Talk with God--Ponder this reading and share your thoughts with God. Listen so that the Holy Spirit might fill you with wisdom and peace. What concrete actions do you need to take based on what God is saying to you?

Highlights from Chapter 2
Seek Renewal

1. There is not a set timeframe for renewing your life after divorce.

2. Three things are important to renewing your life after divorce: finding positive ways to adapt to the realities that result from divorce, finding empowerment to heal, and actively pursuing a positive new direction.

3. One moment at a time, you can begin to let go of the past and start to embrace the changes of your life. God will support you through this process.

4. Deciding which things are within your control and letting go of things that are not, frees you to apply your energies to those areas where you can make things better.

5. You may have to choose to do what is rational rather than what feels right at the moment.

6. When faced with a choice, prayerfully analyzing the risks, barriers, and options can help you make the best decision.

7. Growth requires change, but it also brings opportunity.

8. Prayer gives you a direct line to the greatest resource available. Believe when you pray.

9. Believing that you've missed the best in life keeps you from being open to God's endless possibilities.

10. Assessing responsibilities, priorities, and finances can jump-start you on your way to managing the realities of your new life.

Refuse to live a life flattened by disappointment. Jesus died for you. That's a lot of love and compassion for your well-being.

Stir a passion deep inside and be determined to have the awesome life Jesus died to give you.

CHAPTER 3

UNTIE THE
EMOTIONAL KNOT

As tempting as it may be, brushing emotions away does not lead to peace.

The adage that refers to marriage as, "tying the knot" has a parallel in divorce of untying the knot. Yet untying the emotional knot is seldom easy. Breaking lingering ties requires effort, but is critical to moving forward with your life.

The Emotional Divorce versus the Legal Divorce

There is a time for everything,
and a season for every activity under heaven…

Ecclesiastes 3:1 NIV

Like the legal divorce, the emotional divorce is a process but the ending is not as defined. The emotional divorce evolves as you let go of emotional attachments to your spouse. It occurs when the realities of your marriage and divorce no longer have emotional power in your life.

The timing of the emotional divorce has very little to do with the court date for the legal divorce. However, if legal divorce is your reality, then completing the emotional divorce is important to moving on with life. Because of the different roles each plays in the ending of the marriage, spouses generally are not at the same place in the emotional divorce at the same time, unless the decision to separate is a mutual one.

For some couples, like Michael and Susan, the emotional divorce on the part of at least one person is what leads to the legal divorce. Michael had been unhappy in his marriage for some time. He did not find the relationship fulfilling and even felt that Susan neglected him. He played the role, but over several years, he gradually lost attachment to his wife. He struggled with guilt but began to develop a roving eye. He was miserable, but kept his misery to himself. The situation continued to decline until he decided that he would be happiest living without his wife. When he announced he would be leaving, he felt guilt, but he also felt relief.

People like Michael have likely been dealing with the emotions associated with the breakdown of their marriages for some time before saying they want to divorce. These people may still have a great deal of pain and guilt, but they are likely further into untying the emotional knot than people like Susan who are blindsided by the announcement that their marriages will be ending. This can make someone who has decided to end the marriage relationship seem very cold and unfeeling to the person who is being left. Conversely, it can make the person who is left seem overly emotional to the person who has decided to end the marriage.

After the shock wears off, the person in Susan's role begins the process of adjustment and acceptance. Odds are that the person who got a head start with the emotional divorce has a better chance of emotionally letting go of the marriage before the legal divorce. Other people may not work through the emotional divorce until well after the legal divorce. The tables may turn if the person who decided to end the marriage reevaluates the decision to divorce about the time the person who was left accepts the divorce decision.

Michael and Susan illustrate one way in which emotional divorces may differ. People and situations are not all the same. Nonetheless, knowing there can be differing cycles to the emotional divorce can help you to understand why some of your spouse's behaviors may seem bizarre given what you are currently experiencing.

Completing the Emotional Divorce

Covering over divorce wounds does not help them heal. Completing the emotional divorce involves getting real with your emotions in a way that deals with and then puts to rest the stresses of your marriage and divorce. The following story is a perfect analogy.

Our daughter stepped on broken glass at a pool when she was in high school. Shards of glass were removed from the bottom of her foot. She limped for a while but the wounds healed over in time. Several years later, she began to experience soreness in that foot. Inspection revealed a fragment of glass working its way out of her body. She had suffered a trauma from broken glass years before. Because the wound had not been sufficiently cleaned, it healed over hiding a piece of glass. Eventually, that glass surfaced.

Intentionally working through your emotional divorce is much like that. If you don't sufficiently clean out the wound of divorce, shards of your broken marriage will eventually resurface. No matter how long it takes to probe and clean out your divorce wounds and work through your emotional divorce, do it with commitment and do it thoroughly. Work diligently through this book. If needed, join a support group, or seek counseling.

Making Information and Ideas Work for You

1. How does your role in the ending of your marriage relate to where you are in your emotional divorce?

2. What resources do you need to seek to help you work through the emotional divorce?

Talk with God--Ponder this reading and share your thoughts with God. Listen so that the Holy Spirit might fill you with wisdom and peace. What concrete actions do you need to take based on what God is saying to you?

What is Real

...preserve sound judgment and discernment, do not let them out of your sight; they will be life for you....

Proverbs 3:21 NIV

A sixteen-year old exchange student came to the United States for a year of high school just prior to war breaking out in his home country. Suddenly, contact with, and financial support from his family was dramatically restricted. The atrocities and ravages of war were taking their toll on his relatives and homeland.

As I drove him to an attorney's office to pursue appropriate legal permission to continue school in this country, I empathized with his dilemma. The maturity of his response stopped me in my tracks. He simply said, "It is what is real."

A key to renewing yourself after divorce is to identify and accept what is real. Only when you accept the truths of your situation can you begin to let go of the past and move forward with your life. A good way to enhance your progress on the road to peace is to get a realistic view of your former spouse. Getting real about your former spouse can save you from two distorted views--The Villain View and the Prince or Princess View.

The Villain View

This view focuses completely on your former spouse's faults and misdoings. Odds are that your former spouse is not 100% rotten. Living your life with The Villain View of your former spouse is prone to feed your anger and resentment and to hold you in emotional bondage. The Villain View gives your former spouse emotional power in your current life.

The Prince or Princess View

More like a fairy tale than reality, this view frames your former spouse as the most wonderful and perfect person you can imagine--leaving you to feel you will never find another as good. Even if your relationship can be reconciled, this view is fraught with pitfalls and is almost certain to lead to disappointment. A person may have many good attributes, but romanticizing your mate in this way is not realistic. This unrealistic view keeps you looking back rather than moving forward.

Getting a Realistic View of Your Marriage

Sometimes the dream of the ideal marriage is harder to let go of than the truth of a marriage. You can end up hanging on to something that never was. If you feel that your marriage was a great marriage, but your friends say they are surprised the marriage lasted so long, that discrepancy may be reason to work on getting a grip on the truths of your marriage relationship.

Making Information and Ideas Work

1. Look at your timeline in Chapter 2 and reflect on your relationship with your spouse. Make a list of the good things and the bad things about your spouse. Remember why you fell in love with your spouse. Remember the things that really annoyed you. List as many as you can think of over the next week but be sure to list at least 5 good and 5 bad.

Good Things	*Bad Things*

2. What have you learned from completing these lists?

3. How do the key points in today's reading relate to your life as you reflect on your answers to number 1?

Talk with God--Ponder this reading and share your thoughts with God. Listen so that the Holy Spirit might fill you with wisdom and peace. What concrete actions do you need to take based on what God is saying to you?

Feelings about Your Former Spouse

But I will sing of your strength, in the morning
I will sing of your love; for you are my fortress,
my refuge in times of trouble.

Psalm 59:16 NIV

Divorce proceedings untie the legal knot of marriage, but emotional knots can be much more difficult to untangle. Strong emotional attachments to your former spouse, either positive or negative, can keep you tied to the past in an unhealthy way. Clinging to remnants of a marriage that is obviously over keeps you from moving forward with your life.

Whether emotional ties are feelings of love, concern, need, or resentment, they give the person who is now no longer your spouse, emotional power over you. It may take time, but you can choose to stop yielding that power to your former spouse. To do this you need to identify your emotional knots and work through them until you feel neutral about your former spouse.

A State of Neutral

Feeling neutral means you no longer have strong positive or negative emotions about your former spouse. It does not mean you wish them ill. A state of neutral means you have cut the emotional strings that bind you to the past. Cutting those strings frees you to focus your emotional energy on a positive future. Feeling neutral does not happen all at once, but we believe it is in most circumstances an attainable goal. Achieving a state of neutral takes time and work.

Identify Your Emotional Ties

Identifying emotional ties and understanding how they hold you back can help you to loosen their grip. Thinking through those things that bind you to your former spouse may be hard, but it can also be liberating. The examples in this section represent some emotional ties that may exist.

I'm Worried about My Former Spouse

A burden of worry about your former spouse may mean you are still assuming responsibility for your former spouse's welfare. You may still have concerns, but you are no longer responsible for that person's well-being. If your worry comes from feelings of guilt, know that Christ died so that those who truly regret misdoings and change their ways would not have to carry a burden of worry and guilt.

I Need My Former Spouse's Help

Divorce means you need to assume responsibility for chores your spouse used to handle when you were married. When you need help with things you cannot do for yourself, get help from someone beside your former spouse. Ideally, you and your former spouse will still work together for the direct good of your children.

I'm Too Angry to Let Go

Entrenched anger is an anchor around your neck that weighs you down and ties you firmly to the past. Anger is every bit as much of an emotional tie as is love.

I Wish He Would Just Change

If your spouse would not change when you were married, it is not likely that the changes you wish for will occur once you are divorced.

I Like it That My Former Spouse Won't Let Go

It may be flattering if your former spouse wants to talk with you every day, but it does not help either of you to succeed in breaking with the past. Ask yourself if reconciliation is a realistic possibility. If not, you may find it helpful to set limits on the frequency of your interactions. Otherwise, you are keeping yourself tied to your former spouse.

I Still Feel Married

Ask yourself what feelings, thoughts, and actions are leading you to feel married to someone to whom you are no longer married?

I Don't Feel Whole

Recovering from divorce includes learning to have a sense of well-being in the absence of your former spouse.

I Need to Make My Former Spouse Pay

The need for revenge is an outgrowth of anger. Revenge keeps your focus on your former spouse rather than on your own growth.

Identifying emotional ties to your former spouse is the first step toward working through them. Intentionally working through and letting go of emotional ties is liberating. With work and prayer, it is possible over time to find freedom from emotional ties to the past and to find a satisfying sense of self after marriage and divorce.

Making Information and Ideas Work

1. In what ways do you remain emotionally tied to your former spouse?

2. What needs are you fulfilling by clinging to remnants of your marriage?

3. How can you meet those needs in a more constructive way?

4. What would be the benefits of feeling neutral about your former spouse?

5. List three steps you can take to help yourself break emotional ties to your former spouse.

Talk with God--Ponder this reading and share your thoughts with God. Listen so that the Holy Spirit might fill you with wisdom and peace. What concrete actions do you need to take based on what God is saying to you?

If I Just Knew Why

Peace I leave with you; my peace I give you.
I do not give to you as the world gives.
Do not let your hearts be troubled and do not be afraid.

John 14:27 NIV

"If she'd just tell me why she left," says Todd.

For several years, Todd had stewed over this question. His desperate need to make sense out of his wife's decision to leave their marriage had kept him from completing his emotional divorce. Worse yet, focusing his energies on this nagging question kept him from experiencing the peace offered to him by God.

The question Todd asks is a logical and fair question. He wonders if something he did or didn't do prompted his wife to leave. Or was it something beyond his control? Answers to these questions would be very revealing and could help to shed light on the whys of the breakdown of the marriage. The answers might also lead Todd to better choices in future relationships.

The most significant person in Todd's life decided to end his marriage and she will not explain why. That is no doubt disconcerting. Perhaps she doesn't care to explain, or maybe she doesn't fully understand her reasons herself. Either way, the problem does not belong to Todd's former wife--it belongs to Todd. To have peace, Todd must shift his focus to what he can control.

The difficulty arises in this type of situation when the need to understand is so persistent that it continues to tie a divorcing person emotionally to his former spouse or marriage. Dwelling on the question of why your spouse ended the marriage is self-defeating because the answers may never come. The solution is to make the choice to let go of the question.

Are You Like Todd in Some Way?

Choosing to dwell on a question that will not be answered is choosing to let your heart be troubled. What's more, by continuing to focus on the question, you are giving your former mate control in your life. You are setting yourself up for frustration rather than peace.

Continuing to wonder about something, when no answer is forth coming, is like beating your head against the wall—there is no good purpose in it. Even so, letting go of the need to know may take time, determination, and prayer. Set your mind and heart on letting it go. Give your stress to God. Every time you find yourself questioning why, talk to yourself and God about your thinking:

> I'm wondering why again.
> Wondering why is futile and painful.
> Here, God, you take it away.
> I choose your peace instead.

Say this every time you find yourself asking why. God is willing to free you of the why question the first time you ask, but you may need to retrain your brain to stop asking the question. Keep at it until you let go of the why question and accept the peace that God promises.

Making Information and Ideas Work

1. Am I struggling with a need to get an answer that my former spouse is not willing or able to give? What is the question?

2. How is struggling with this question affecting me?

3. How can I reflect on the ideas I just read in *If I Just Knew Why* and apply them to my situation in a way that will make my life better?

Talk with God--Ponder this reading and share your thoughts with God. Listen so that the Holy Spirit might fill you with wisdom and peace. What concrete actions do you need to take based on what God is saying to you?

Speed Bumps, Potholes, and Roadblocks

Come to me, all you who are weary and burdened,
and I will give you rest.

Matthew 11:28 NIV

Traveling the road to the emotional divorce is easier if
you know about the barriers you might encounter along the
way. Emotional barriers on this journey are often rooted in
wrong thinking. That means you have the power to change
your thinking and overcome these emotional barriers.
Whether barriers are speed bumps, potholes or full-fledged
roadblocks depends on your success in getting beyond them.

The first step is to recognize barriers when they appear.
The second step is to identify the thinking that creates the
barrier. The third step is to replace barrier thinking with
healthier thinking.

Barriers to the Emotional Divorce

Below are six examples of barriers that may block or
slow an emotional divorce.

1. Pretending You're Fine When You Are Not
Barrier Belief: If I pretend I'm okay, I will be okay.
Healthier Belief: I need to work through my grief and
other emotions. If I allow the pain to surface, then I can
work through it in a healthy way and get beyond it.

The Truth: Putting on a happy face when you are hurting inside is like putting a bunny suit on a dog—cotton-tail or not, it is still a dog. Hiding your emotions does not make them disappear, and can in fact, make you ill. On the other hand, feeling and processing feelings allows you to move beyond them.

2. *Feeling, Thinking, and Acting Angry*

Barrier Belief: Living in anger provides a balance to the injustice done to me.

Healthier Belief: My anger may be justified, but it hurts me more than anyone else.

The Truth: Blaming others, even when they are guilty, diverts your attention from taking responsibility for your own healing. Anger can create an internal pressure that becomes explosive. This may prompt acting in ways that vent the pressure but have negative outcomes.

3. *Looking for Someone to Replace Your Spouse*

Barrier Belief: The quickest and best way to fill the emptiness inside is with another romantic relationship.

Healthier Belief: Getting involved with someone before I work through my emotions is a recipe for an unsuccessful new relationship.

Truth: By developing friendships, and getting involved in organizations, support groups, or volunteer work, you can help fill the relationship void in your life. These relationships, more than a romantic relationship, allow time to work through your separation and divorce. By healing first, you will be more prepared for a romantic relationship in the future.

4. *Escaping by Staying Overly Busy or by Using Alcohol or Drugs to Numb the Pain*

Barrier Belief: Escaping thoughts and feelings about my divorce relieves the hurt.

Healthier Belief: Escaping just delays the work I need to do to move past my divorce.

Truth: Staying busy or using alcohol may help you to escape temporarily, but if you use these activities to avoid the issues of your divorce, those issues will likely resurface.

5. *Dwelling on Things You Cannot Change*

Barrier Belief: If I dwell on a problem, I can make sense of it.

Healthier Belief: If I accept the reality of those things, and accept that they may never make sense to me, I can then use my energy to build myself a more joyful life.

Truth: Dwelling on something you cannot change is a waste of energy. Choosing to dwell on your problems keeps you from taking responsibility for making your life better.

6. *Not Forgiving*

Barrier Belief: My spouse does not deserve forgiveness.

Healthier Belief: Forgiving is not the same as approving of behavior. Forgiving my former spouse lifts the burden of resentment from my spirit.

*Truth***:** Forgiving someone else is not about your relationship with that person. It is about your relationship with yourself and God.

The Not-So-Merry-Go-Round

Failure to work past barriers puts you on a not-so-merry-go-round. Rather than moving forward, you get stuck going around and around. Working through barriers breaks the circle. Seeking the Lord's help in the process helps lift the burden.

Taking Charge of Barriers

With self-reflection, determination, and prayer, you can tear down barriers to finding peace after divorce. When you find you are struggling with unhealthy beliefs, stop and identify new healthier beliefs. If you repeat this process over time, you increase your chance of internalizing these healthier beliefs. Chapter 6 covers more about how beliefs and thoughts influence the ability to find peace after divorce. Additionally, various sections of this book delve into more detail about the barriers given as examples in this section.

Making Information and Ideas Work

1. What barriers to healing from divorce do you recognize in your own life?

2. What are the underlying beliefs you have that support each of your barriers?

3. What healthier beliefs might you adopt to help you get past your barriers?

Talk with God--Ponder this reading and share your thoughts with God. Listen so that the Holy Spirit might fill you with wisdom and peace. What concrete actions do you need to take based on what God is saying to you?

Make a Defining Break

But Lot's wife looked back,
and she became a pillar of salt.

Genesis 19:26 NIV

Lot is warned to flee with his family because God is going to destroy the sinful city where he lives. He is told, "Don't look back, and don't stop anywhere in the plain!" Unfortunately, Lot's wife looks back. Evidently, she finds it hard to leave the life she knows best. By looking back, she becomes a symbol of all of us who are reluctant to let go of the past and move on to where God is leading us.

As hard as it is, and it is hard, moving forward from divorce means letting go of past entanglements. Whether or not the divorce was your idea, moving yourself forward after the breakup of a marriage is a challenge. The person who is still clinging to the marriage may struggle to accept that it is over and may look for ways to stay connected to the former, or soon-to-be-former, spouse. The person who decided to end the marriage may make nice to the person who was left in an effort to feel less guilty. Such acts of kindness may be mistakenly be interpreted by the person who was left as hope of reconciliation.

If you make every effort to reconcile and the marriage cannot survive, then making a defining break in your relationship with your former spouse can be important to your ability to move on with your life. This is especially advantageous as you work on your emotional divorce. A defining break helps establish your identities as two independent individuals.

Prolonging the process of letting go of your spouse complicates the dynamics of your new relationship as two people who are no longer married to each other. Since moving beyond divorce means letting go, making a defining break rather than dragging it out makes sense. Going out to dinner together, talking about your day with one another, constant texting or talking on the phone, relying on your former spouse, having sexual relations with each other, all prevent letting go and hinder your ability to find a new life.

When Children are a Part of the Picture

Parenting creates an added dimension to making a defining break. Contact with your former spouse still needs to exist for the good of the children. The challenge is to keep interactions civil and centered on the well-being of the children and still re-define your relationship as two independent adults.

I Want to Be Friends with My Former Spouse

Whether or not you decide to create a defining break is up to you. We have observed that those who do choose a defining break find it easier to move on with their lives. Once a couple's relationship is re-defined as one of two independent adults, it appears there is a better chance of having a cordial relationship that is not confused by the past.

Another potential risk to hanging on to your former spouse, even when reconciliation is not possible, is that it has the potential to interfere with future relationships. Think about it. Would you want to become romantically involved with someone who is still close to a former spouse? Probably not.

A Lesson from a Lizard

One morning I watched as a small lizard struggled between the panes of an open window. With one leg, he held on for dear life to the wood between the panes of glass as his other legs struggled in vain to move him upward between the two sashes. The fit of the sashes closed him out completely. No amount of effort to hang on would ever be able to get him anywhere. The only productive solution was to let go. The lizard had to sever his relationship with the piece of wood or he would have been putting a lot of energy into a situation with no future.

You too will be putting energy into a situation with no future if you persist in maintaining ties to a marriage with no

78

hope for reconciliation. Making a defining break can be hard. Yet a defining break will allow you to put more energy into your own healing and future.

Making Information and Ideas Work

1. What points in today's reading are most relevant to you?

2. What do you need to do to make a more defined break with your former spouse?

Talk with God--Ponder this reading and share your thoughts with God. Listen so that the Holy Spirit might fill you with wisdom and peace. What concrete actions do you need to take based on what God is saying to you?

Emotional Flare-Ups

*May the God of hope fill you with all joy
and peace as you trust in him,
so that you may overflow with hope
by the power of the Holy Spirit.*

Romans 15:13 NIV

One minute I was laughing at the movie. The next minute, my eyes began to well with tears even though everyone else in the theatre was still laughing. A man in the movie said something that made me remember a sadness regarding my former marriage. To everyone else it was funny. For me it caused an unexpected emotional flare-up on an otherwise good day. I cried for several minutes, stuffed away my tissues, and felt better. Over time, as I continued to work through my divorce, emotional flare-ups eventually went away.

Emotional flare-ups are normal for those recovering from divorce. The smell of your former spouse's cologne, a song, or any number of things that stimulate a memory may blindside you with a surge in emotions. Emotional flare-ups can happen at the most unexpected times, even after you think you are okay. Realize they are normal, allow yourself to feel them, cry if that is what you feel like doing.

Special Times

It is not surprising to experience a flare-up of emotions during the holidays or on anniversaries. Times that were special times with your former mate may initially be difficult when by yourself. Planning these times to minimize emotional distress, especially if children are involved, can help to ease the adjustment.

Anticipating a first holiday may in fact be more stressful than the actual day once it comes. As much as it is possible, relax and allow first holidays and anniversaries to come and go. Over the coming years you can decide what old traditions to keep and as a matter of course, create new traditions and new memories. The joy can once again return to these occasions.

The Dimmer

The emotions associated with divorce are not turned off with the flick of a switch, but rather with a dimmer. That's okay because it allows you time to work through the emotional and lifestyle shifts you must make. Emotional flare-ups, both unexpected and anticipated will likely occur. Prepare yourself. As you prayerfully continue to work through emotional flare-ups, they are likely to reduce in frequency and intensity.

Making Information and Ideas Work

1. Have you been blind-sided by an emotional flare-up?

2. How do you deal with emotional flare-ups?

3. What special events such as holidays or anniversaries are most difficult for you?

4. What steps can you take to increase your peace when coping with these special events?

Talk with God--Ponder this reading and share your thoughts with God. Listen so that the Holy Spirit might fill you with wisdom and peace. What concrete actions do you need to take based on what God is saying to you?

Highlights from Chapter 3
Untie the Emotional Knot

1. Processing your emotions allows you to work through them until they lose their power to tie you in an unhealthy way to your former marriage.

2. The emotional divorce evolves as you let go of emotional attachments to your spouse and begin to identify yourself as single. The emotional divorce occurs when the issues of your marriage and divorce no longer have emotional power in your life.

3. Because of the different roles each plays in the ending of the marriage, spouses generally are not at the same emotional place at the same time.

4. No matter how long it takes to work through your emotional divorce, do it with commitment and do it thoroughly.

5. An unrealistic view of your marriage relationship or of your former spouse can hinder your ability to find peace.

6. Emotional ties, both positive and negative, give the person who is now no longer your spouse emotional power over you.

7. Feeling neutral means you no longer have strong feelings, positive or negative about your former spouse. It does not mean you wish them ill.

8. Working through and letting go of emotional ties to your former spouse can help you to move beyond your divorce and on to freedom and a satisfying sense of yourself.

9. When you find your thinking is creating a barrier to finding peace after divorce, stop and identify a healthier thought.

10. Emotional flare-ups during separation and divorce are normal. Feel them, accept them, and then move on.

11. Make plans for holidays that will ease necessary breaks with old traditions. Relax and enjoy.

12. Prolonging the process of letting go of your spouse may complicate your ability to move forward with your life.

13. Making as definitive a break as possible with your former spouse can allow you to put more energy into your own healing and future.

14. You may never get desired answers from your former spouse.

15. To nurture a sense of peace, shift your focus to what you can control.

16. Gaining a realistic view of your former spouse and marriage helps you move on with your life.

17. Getting real with your emotions is important to helping break emotional ties. Breaking emotional ties allows for forward movement in your life.

CHAPTER 4

LOOK INSIDE

Taking a good look inside can help you know where you are so you can find ways to move to where you want to go.

Know thyself is a Greek adage that sums up a lot of wisdom in two simple words. Knowing yourself allows you to build on your strengths and grow in areas that need growth. Knowing yourself gives you a platform for healing the wounds of divorce. Taking a good look inside can help you know where you are so you can find ways to move to where you want to go.

Fear

So do not fear, for I am with you; do not be dismayed, for
I am your God. I will strengthen you and help you;
I will uphold you with my righteous right hand.

Isaiah 41:10 NIV

Divorce with all of its uncertainties can be scary. Nothing is quite as fear provoking as instability combined with an unknown future. Fear fuels anxiety about the present and the future. If not addressed, fears may persist for years after the legal marriage is over.

Fear is not always bad. A healthy response to fear can be lifesaving by inspiring departure from an abusive relationship. Fear can keep you from making choices that have negative outcomes. The ability to fear is a gift from God.

When you allow fear to dominate your life, the tables turn. Fear is no longer life giving–it is life taking. When you live in fear, you subject yourself to worry, anxiety, dread, and discouragement.

Fear keeps you from seeing possibilities and making the choices needed to better your life. Physical spin-offs of fear such as tension, stomachaches, and headaches may also plague you. If anxiety and fear override faith, suffering increases.

Putting Fear into Perspective

You can feed fear with thoughts about all of the bad things that could happen, or you can instead choose to put situations into perspective. Gaining perspective entails getting real about the things that scare you and understanding the truth about fear. It also requires looking at your choices about fear.

The Things That Scare

Quite often, fear tricks the mind into magnifying potential dangers. Concerns become bigger than reality as you dwell on them. Such fears may become paralyzing.

By stepping back from these fears and assessing their realities, you get a grip on the truth of situations. Truth is freeing since it helps you let go of unwarranted anxiety, and break through the paralysis of fear. A realistic understanding of the risks and opportunities of a scary situation can empower you to make informed choices, to avoid dangers, and to act for positive outcomes.

Sources of Anxieties and Fears
Cited by After Divorce Ministries
Workshop Participants

The unknown	The future
Living life alone	Self-worth
Financial security	New responsibilities
Starting over	Coping with family
Dating again	Single parenting

The Truth about Fear

Getting a grip on fear means not only gaining a realistic view of what frightens you, it also means replacing fear with faith. When fears surface, you have a choice. You can allow fear to keep a grip on you, or you can get a grip on fear. Allowing a fear to keep a grip on you will lead to worry, anxiety, discouragement, and timidity. Choosing faith instead allows you to get a grip on fear as God strengthens you and holds you up victorious. Faith in God gives power, love, self-discipline, and encouragement (Isaiah 41:10 and 2 Timothy 1:7 NIV). Fear sees the danger in the unknown. Faith in God sees the possibilities in the unknown. You have the power to choose to feed fear, or feed faith.

Interestingly Proverbs 9:10, says, "The Fear of the LORD is the beginning of wisdom, and knowledge of the Holy One is understanding." In this context, the word fear suggests a holy respect for the power and authority of the Lord. Respect for the Lord and a relationship with him can help us overcome fears related to divorce as well as all of the other paralyzing fears we face in life.

Courage in the Face of Fear

Faith in God is a bridge. It crosses the gap between the paralysis of fear, and the courage to act in the face of fear. Even when you are scared and don't have much confidence in yourself, confidence in God provides the strength to do what is needed. Armed with God-based courage, you can step up to the challenges of divorce. Looking fear in the face and challenging it with truth and with the Word of God, you can press on through the fear. Then an amazing thing happens--the power of the fear diminishes. Prayerfully pushing through the fears that spring from divorce is empowering.

Worry, Fear, and Anxiety Meet Prayer

Prayer strengthens the God-based courage that comes with faith. When worry, fear, and anxiety meet prayer, they subside. Paul tells about this in Philippians 4:5-7.

> *The Lord is near. Do not be anxious about anything, but in everything, by prayer and petition, with thanksgiving, present your requests to God. And the peace of God which transcends all understanding, will guard your hearts and your minds in Christ Jesus.*

This scripture gives a three-step guide to developing a life of faith rather than one of fear.

- Remember that the Lord is near.
- Replace anxiety by talking with God.
- With a thankful heart, tell God your needs. God promises to guard your heart and mind in Christ Jesus and give you peace.

Fear in a Nutshell

Fear can keep you safe, but living in fear is debilitating. Knowing the truth about things that scare you can help keep fears from spinning out of control. Looking fear in the face and challenging it with truth and with the truth of the Word of God, allows you to press on through the fear. Then an amazing thing happens--the power of the fear diminishes.

It is the promise of Psalm 34:4, "I sought the Lord, and he answered me; he delivered me from all my fears."

> *Peace I leave with you; my peace I give you. I do not give to you as the world gives. Do not let your hearts be troubled and do not be afraid.*
>
> John 14:27 NIV

Making Information and Ideas Work

1. Think of your most haunting divorce-related fear. Write that fear below.

2. What is the reality of the situation as it relates to this fear? How likely is your fear to become a reality? If it does, what is the worst that could happen?

3. What thoughts and beliefs would help you neutralize this fear?

4. What healthy action do you need to take to make something positive occur regarding this fear?

5. What are you feeding in your spirit--fear or faith? How?

Talk with God--Ponder this reading and share your thoughts with God. Listen so that the Holy Spirit might fill you with wisdom and peace. What concrete actions do you need to take based on what God is saying to you?

Guilt and Regrets

"Pick me up and throw me into the sea," he replied, "and it will become calm. I know that it is my fault that this great storm has come upon you."

Jonah 1:12 NIV

Jonah knew without a doubt that he was guilty of running from God and of failing to do what God told him to do. His guilt was causing consequences, not only for himself, but for others as well. When he owned up to his guilt, he still had to deal with the consequence of being thrown into the sea, but he also moved himself a step closer to God.

In a similar way, owning up to the ways you contributed to your divorce does not eliminate the consequences, but it can bring you closer to God and can clear your conscience. Sitting in a whale with his head wrapped in seaweed and his life fading away, Jonah chose to call on God. God rescued him from death not because Jonah deserved it but because God is a God of grace.

Feeling Guilty over Divorce?

The most justified reasons for true divorce-related guilt involve violation of the marriage vows. Have you failed to love, honor and keep? Have you been unfaithful? Have you neglected your spouse? Have you been physically or emotionally abusive? Have you abandoned your spouse? Identifying the reasons for your feelings of guilt can help you process them and prepare yourself to ask God for forgiveness and healing.

Accept God's Forgiveness

If you are carrying guilt, know that God will forgive you if you sincerely ask. For some, accepting God's forgiveness is hard, but remember, God does not forgive you because you are good--he forgives you because he is good. "If we confess our sins, he is faithful and just and will forgive us our sins and purify us from all unrighteousness" (1John 1:9).

That means that God not only forgives you, but that he will help you to grow into a better person who is closer to him. Failure to accept God's forgiveness is to suggest that Jesus died in vain. God already offers you forgiveness. He wants you to accept his offer.

Good News

You will still have to cope with the natural consequences of your choices, but you do not have to carry the heavy load of guilt that burdens your soul. Furthermore, nothing can separate you from the love of God. Paul says, "For I am convinced that neither death nor life, neither angels nor demon, neither the present nor the future, nor any powers, neither height nor depth, nor anything else in all creation, will be able to separate us from the love of God that is in Christ Jesus our Lord" (Romans 8:38-39 NIV). "Anything else in all creation," must surely include divorce. Accept God's forgiveness and forgive yourself as well. God will help you heal from your sorrow day by day as you take an active role in dealing with your new circumstances.

The Corinthians learned that turning to God when they were in distress helped them to have a more positive spirit. They became "...more alive, more concerned, more sensitive, more reverent, more human, more passionate, more responsible" (2 Corinthians 7:11-13, The Message). They came through their distress with "purity of heart." Paul praises them and points out that turning to God is a good choice in a time of sorrow and regret. Turning away from God leaves us to carry our guilt and regrets, on our own, for the rest of our lives.

Forgive Yourself

Continuing to beat yourself up over mistakes, may make you feel like you are paying for what you did wrong. Actually, all you are doing is bogging down in something for which Christ has already cancelled the debt. Not forgiving yourself is equal to not accepting God's forgiveness. Concentrate your energies on accepting God's forgiveness, and then ask God what he would have you learn from your mistakes.

Feelings of guilt as they relate to the breakdown of your marriage can create a heavy weight to bear. Sometimes, the feelings of guilt are justified and sometimes they are not. It is important to make this distinction. The dynamics that lead to the end of a marriage can be very complicated and things are not always black and white.

If you are an abused spouse who feels guilty for causing the abuse you received, you are carrying unmerited guilt. Nothing you did or did not do justifies abuse. Abuse is a violation of the marriage vows and is just cause for divorce.

A different example of unmerited guilt comes from a woman who participated in one of our workshops. Despite the years of neglect she endured from her husband, she felt guilty for filing for divorce. Reflecting on her situation after her divorce was final, she says, "It sounds odd to say God gave me the strength to leave my husband, but he did."

If you are blaming yourself unfairly, give yourself a break. If you are responsible for things you regret, humbly ask God's forgiveness; find the lesson in what you've done; hold on to that wisdom; accept God's forgiveness and forgive yourself. Move on.

Regret

Sometimes, feelings of sadness over what happened in a marriage are based on regret rather than guilt. Regret is simply when you wish things had been different. Perhaps you regret things you did or things you feel you should have done.

You may also regret things related to circumstances that are not really anyone's fault. For example, you may regret outcomes related to less than desirable economic influences or the unfortunate timing of certain events. It is important to work through guilt and regrets. The following six steps may prove helpful.

6 Steps for Dealing with Guilt and Regrets

1. Acknowledge regrets and guilt to God and ask his forgiveness.
2. Change what you can.
3. Accept what is now beyond your control.
4. Release regrets and guilt to God.
5. Ask God what he wants you to learn from your experiences.
6. Allow yourself to heal and grow.

God forgives you the first time you ask. Repeat the above steps as many times as needed until you forgive yourself.

Making Information and Ideas Work

1. What feelings of guilt are you still carrying regarding the breakdown of your marriage?

2. Look back at the timeline you made in the section en-titled, *Moving from Acceptance to Renewal.* Look at the

times that represent the most negative memories in your marriage. For each of those times, make a list of things you wish you had done differently.

3. How do you feel about asking God for forgiveness?

4. What steps do you need to take to forgive yourself?

5. Reflect on your timeline again. What regrets do you have regarding circumstances?

Talk with God--Ponder this reading and share your thoughts with God. Listen so that the Holy Spirit might fill you with wisdom and peace. What concrete actions do you need to take based on what God is saying to you?

Rejection and Vulnerability

Fear of man will prove to be a snare, but whoever trusts in the LORD is kept safe.

Proverbs 29:25 NIV

"I'm 43 years old and I've spent my entire life wanting other people to tell me I'm okay," says Claire. First, it was my father. To this day, I still look to him to give me some sort of positive feedback. I don't think he ever will. Next, it was my husband, but he never helped me to feel like I was worthwhile either. Now to top it off, he wants a divorce."

Feelings of rejection are understandably strong when your mate walks out the door. If you lived with someone who is neglectful, distant, or abusive, you may have experience rejection for some time. The experience of rejection gives a piercing blow right to the heart of your self-worth.

That someone no longer loves you does not mean that you are not loveable. That someone no longer values you does not mean that you are not valuable. The God of all creation loves and values you very much.

Many different influences can go into someone's decision to leave a marriage. Not all of them have to do with the merits of the individual who is left. Outside influences, family history, and even the self-esteem of the departing person can be among the contributing factors. It does not necessarily mean that either party in the divorce is a bad person.

If your former partner dishes out demeaning comments, it can further your sense of rejection. Repeated putdowns can result in feelings of inferiority. Take comfort in knowing that harsh words and behaviors say more about the person dishing them out than they do about the person who is receiving them. Do not give another person the power to make you feel bad about yourself.

Believing you are unworthy because your spouse rejected you or treated you poorly is allowing the actions of that person to put a fear in your heart that perhaps you really may be unworthy. As Proverbs 29:25 states, that fear "will prove to be a snare." Accepting the idea that you are unworthy opens you to a host of vulnerabilities. Do not allow anyone to convince you that you are unworthy.

You are worthy when you are a child of God. That is why Proverbs also states that, "whoever trusts in the Lord is kept safe." Trusting that God values you restores your sense of worth and protects you from falling prey to the snare of human judgments.

Claire says she has now had an, "ah-ha moment," and realizes that she needs to spend time learning to feel good about herself from the inside. By doing so, she will be able to feel good about herself without allowing her self-worth to depend on other people. "I've never done that for myself. I've always looked to other people to tell me I'm worth something. It's time I work on feeling good about myself."

Making Information and Ideas Work

1. How can you not let someone else make you feel inferior?

2. How do the points in this section on rejection relate to your life?

3. What does the Bible say about your value to God?

Talk with God--Ponder this reading and share your thoughts with God. Listen so that the Holy Spirit might fill you with wisdom and peace. What concrete actions do you need to take based on what God is saying to you?

> *That someone no longer loves you does not*
> *mean that you are not loveable.*
> *That someone no longer values you does not*
> *mean that you are not valuable.*
> *The God of all creation loves*
> *and values you very much.*

Loss and Grief

I called on your name, O Lord, from the depths of the pit.
You heard my plea: "Do not close your ears to my cry for
relief." You came near when I called you, and you said,
"Do not fear." O Lord, you took up my case; you
redeemed my life.

Lamentations 3:55-58 NIV

The breakdown of your marriage may leave you feeling like you are in the depths of a pit. You don't have to stay there. God is speaking to you through the book of Lamentations. To you, he says--Do not fear. I will take up your case and redeem your life.

The death of a marriage can create the feeling of being in an earthquake and a hurricane at the same time. Many things are in flux and many of the changes represent loss. Grief is a natural reaction and expressing that grief is healthy.

Jesus expressed grief when he joined mourning friends soon after Lazarus' death. John tells us that Jesus was "deeply moved in spirit and troubled" (John 11:33 NIV). In fact, "Jesus wept" (John 11:35 NIV).

Grieving is a process God gives us to help us heal when something or someone we value is lost. Identifying grief and addressing it is critical; otherwise, grief may drag out for years. Once you realize that what you are feeling is grief, it can be easier to begin the path toward healing. Actively working through your grief is like giving a gift to yourself since doing so will help you to heal.

Working through Grief

Make a deliberate decision to deal with your divorce grief. Grief does not go away on its own. It is important to work through the emotions associated with the losses related to divorce. Doing so takes persistence.

Be patient with yourself. Adding more stress to your life by trying to fit your grief into a certain timeframe serves no purpose. Working through the grief of divorce is a gradual process with no specific finish line that applies to everyone. You will know when your grief is completed.

Don't expect a formula. Not everyone experiences grief in exactly the same way, so don't think you have to force your grief into identified patterns. Allow yourself to grieve in your own way at your own speed.

Find supportive friends. People who will listen without judgment are a great asset. Build a network of these people.

Face the feelings of grief head on. Telling yourself and others that you are fine when you are not does not make the hurt inside go away. Talking and thinking excessively about the events that contributed to your grief, without actually dealing with the emotions of your grief, does not really help you heal either. Unresolved issues left lurking under the surface keep you from having peace and may haunt future relationships.

Allow time in an appropriate place to gush out your emotions daily. Declare your emotions aloud. Find a private place and shout. Pound a punching bag, or run if that helps.

Find a way, time, and place where you can vent and express your grief in an appropriate way that is respectful of others.

Honestly facing your feelings and then working through them can take away the power of those feelings so that you may move forward free of their grip. Here are some questions to help you deal with the grief feelings of divorce as they surface.

- Exactly what emotion am I feeling?
- What triggered that emotion?
- How can I express that emotion appropriately?

Grief and the Divorce-Related Gloomies

Feeling very down over the losses that come with divorce is normal. It may be hard to get a good night's sleep due to conflicting emotions. Thinking may seem scattered and your appetite may be nonexistent or go crazy. Coping with the changes may leave you without much energy.

You may be experiencing what I've dubbed the divorce-related gloomies. The divorce-related gloomies are down feelings associated with the situations of your divorce. (Note: The divorce-related gloomies are not to be confused with depression. Only qualified medical professionals can diagnose and treat depression. Seek their help as needed.)

If you are experiencing the divorce-related gloomies, the good news is that you are likely going through something that many folks experience during the grief of divorce. Being proactive about your renewal after divorce will help you work through the things that contribute to the divorce-related gloomies and allow you to move to a more peaceful place. Much help can be found through prayer, support groups, and counseling.

> *Being proactive about your renewal after divorce will help you work through the things that contribute to the divorce-related gloomies and allow you to move to a more peaceful place.*

Making Information and Ideas Work

1. What relevance do the points in 'Working through Grief' have to your situation?

2. Why is it good to recognize and work through grief?

3. When reflecting on your divorce, what grief or loss related emotion do you find yourself feeling most often?

4. What is behind that emotion? (Be specific)

5. How can you vent that emotion appropriately?

Talk with God--Ponder this reading and share your thoughts with God. Listen so that the Holy Spirit might fill you with wisdom and peace. What concrete actions do you need to take based on what God is saying to you?

Loneliness

The LORD your God is with you, he is mighty to save.
He will take great delight in you, he will quiet you with
his love, he will rejoice over you with singing.

Zephaniah 3:17 NIV

Loneliness of the Heart

"My heart was lonely, even when people were around," said Fred reflecting on his separation and divorce. Like many others, he was experiencing the hollow feeling of heartfelt loneliness that may result from the loss of a former spouse. Such emptiness can result from the loss of the dream of a happy marriage as much as by the loss of a spouse.

Because most people don't relish a lonely heart, there can be a tendency to avoid dealing with it by staying very busy. Activity may provide a distraction and temporarily ease stress, but a reasonable amount of time spent alone may actually help you get over loneliness. Solitude can provide time to work through emotions, thoughts, and beliefs. Feelings of loneliness will likely dissipate as you begin to build a sense of yourself and to define your new life in positive ways. The move from a lonely heart to contentment takes time and a willingness to work through the pain, let go of the past, and look to the future.

Where Did Everybody Go?

Another form of loneliness comes from changes in relationships related to the former marriage. "Her family told me they loved me like a son," said Carl. "Now they have nothing to do with me." In-laws may stay in touch, turn on you, or vanish in a flash.

Friends may also scatter, especially couples. Perhaps it is because they don't know what to say. Maybe they are afraid of the idea that their marriage may also be vulnerable. Others feel like they must choose sides between you and your former spouse. Some who are insecure in their marriages may be threatened by your availability. Whatever the reasons, a shift in your support network is likely to occur and can add to a sense of loneliness. Although this shift may be unsettling at first, it may help you move away from the past and toward establishing yourself as a single person with a life of your own.

Life in Limbo Land

Limbo Land is the awkward time and state of being between separation and divorce. "When you're going through divorce, you feel you don't fit in anywhere," says Jean Henderson. "You are neither single nor a part of a couple."

In Limbo Land, the reality of married life is over and your identity as a married person is vanishing – but you are still legally married. Life is in a major transition. Limbo Land can present challenges even in your church life. As one workshop participant points out, "I no longer feel like I fit with the married group, and I can't join the singles group yet because they require I be unmarried."

Despite its trials, Limbo Land offers a much-needed time for beginning to process life's changes. It is an important time of getting your head together and redefining your life. Embrace Limbo Land as a time to cry out to God, settle your nerves, clear your head, and begin your journey to peace after divorce. Limbo Land will serve its purpose and end, leaving you on your way to a positive new life.

Embracing Limbo Land

Spend Time with Yourself

It is important to realize that being alone does not have to be lonely. Use your alone time to work through grief and to get to know yourself. Make a list of your interests, strengths, and blessings. Consider your goals. Learn to be comfortable with yourself, by yourself. It is an awesome feeling.

Establish Support

Soon after divorce, it may be tempting to stay in a shell and isolate yourself. Continued isolation can become depressing, so balance time alone with time spent with others. By forcing yourself to go out, even when you don't feel like it, you will expose yourself to the refreshing effect of time spent outside your shell.

Family members and long-time friends can be valuable anchors as you process your divorce, but you may need to extend your support network. Joining organizations can help to expand your circle of friends and provide added support. Getting involved with a church is a good way to find fellowship and spiritual support.

Support groups related to divorce recovery can also help, especially if they provide information as well as an opportunity to talk with others who have experienced divorce. Personal counseling is another option. As you establish your support network, be sure to find people who will help you grow. People who pull you down are not candidates for your support network.

It can be easy to overwhelm others with your needs as you work through getting past your divorce, especially if you are a very verbal person. If you are, find more than one person you can talk with so that you don't end up burning out any one friend. You'll get more support.

Go Outside Yourself

Helping others can work wonders for loneliness. It gets you outside of yourself and highlights your worth. It creates a positive impact on you as much as it does on the people you help. Reach out to others on your own, through a church, or by volunteering through a service organization.

A Greater Presence Is with You

Jesus promises, "And surely I am with you always, to the very end of the age" (Matthew 28:20 NIV). Enough said.

Making Information and Ideas Work

1. Where are you on the road to finding contentment in being alone?

2. In what ways can you extend your personal support network?

3. List three avenues for serving others that you would consider exploring. Choose one and identify a plan for getting involved.

4. How can you increase your awareness of the Holy Spirit in your life?

Talk with God--Ponder this reading and share your thoughts with God. Listen so that the Holy Spirit might fill you with wisdom and peace. What concrete actions do you need to take based on what God is saying to you?

*If you love me, you will obey what I command.
And I will ask the Father, and he will give you another
Counselor to be with you forever— the Spirit of truth.
The world cannot accept him,
because it neither sees him nor knows him.
But you know him, for he lives with you and
will be in you.*

John 14:15-17 NIV

The Empty Love Pot

What a man desires is unfailing love...

Proverbs 19:22 NIV

Everybody wants to be loved. The desire to be loved and to love is woven into the fabric of being human. Divorce severs a most significant love relationship and may leave us eager to find love anywhere to fill the emptiness inside.

With an empty love pot, it can be tempting to try to replace the loss with another romance before allowing time to heal from the pains of divorce. The attention, conversation, and touch of a new person make romance particularly attractive. However, jumping into the dating world before being ready is like jumping out of the frying pan into the fire. It is too easy to be burnt again and burns are not as easy to handle when you are already hurting. Building a relationship on the heels of a dissolved or dissolving marriage is like trying to build a home on wobbly stilts. It's risky at best.

Needy people find it more difficult to analyze the realities of a dating relationship. They may say yes when they should say no. Even though logic dictates that the current dating relationship is not likely to work out very well, they may stay in a negative relationship just to avoid the emptiness they know they will feel when yet another relationship falls apart.

Finding peace after divorce is about healing hurts and letting go of the past. It is a time for introspection and finding safe, nurturing relationships. Jumping into dating to fill the void derails the purpose of healing from divorce.

Building internal strength and working through divorce issues before dating will better equip you to make good judgment calls in a dating relationship. It will also provide better footing for handling the risk of rejection and hurt associated with dating.

Before seeking romance, find comfort in safer relationships. Doing so will provide support and fill your love pot resulting in a less vulnerable state once you start to date.
Fill your love pot with the love of God, the love of self (to love others, you must first love yourself), and the love of friends. You will be much more self-assured and better equipped to deal with the ups and downs of dating when the time comes. Fulfilling the desire of human love will be much more within reach if you first allow the perfect and unfailing love of God to heal and empower you.

What if I'm Already Involved with Someone?

Are you ready to be in a new romantic relationship? Now is the time for a heart-to-heart talk with yourself. Pray for insight before answering the reality check questions below. Take a deep breath and get real with yourself.

1. Are you dating this person because you are needy? Are you searching for someone to fill the loneliness or to provide reassurance that you are loveable?

2. Are you using this relationship to try to heal yourself from divorce?

3. Is dating an attempt to prove to your former spouse that you are desirable?

4. Do you tolerate less than respectful behavior from the person you are dating? Do you find that you sometimes say yes when you really feel you should say no? Do you find yourself agreeing with things just to avoid losing the relationship?

5. Have you taken time to fill your love pot with the love of God, the love of self, and the love of friends prior to entering this relationship?

6. Are you dating this person because you now feel confident, whole, and ready to be an equal partner? Have you untied the emotional knot of your previous marriage(s)?

7. Do you have a good sense of yourself as an individual? Have you taken time to discover your own interests and goals since your divorce but prior to this relationship?

8. Can you be true to yourself to the point that you would be willing to let the person you are romantically involved with walk away rather than to sacrifice your sense of self or your values?

Answering *yes* to any of the questions in numbers 1-4 may cast doubt in your mind about your readiness to be in a new relationship. Answering *no* to the questions in numbers 1-4 and *yes* to all of the questions in numbers 5-8, suggests much more solid ground for starting a new romantic relationship. What do your answers to the preceding questions tell you about your readiness to be involved in a romantic relationship?

Making Information and Ideas Work

1. How can neediness affect your ability to make good judgment calls in a dating relationship?

2. Why is it important to fill your divorce-depleted love pot with the love of God, family and friends before becoming involved romantically with someone new?

3. How can allowing God to make you whole improve the quality of your relationships when you date again?

Talk with God--Ponder this reading and share your thoughts with God. Listen so that the Holy Spirit might fill you with wisdom and peace. What concrete actions do you need to take based on what God is saying to you?

Joy and Laughter

...Now is your time of grief, but I will see you again and you will rejoice, and no one will take away your joy.

John 16:22 NIV

Joy versus Happiness

Happiness relates to happenings that occur in your world. If your happening is the breakdown of your marriage, you are probably not happy. Joy on the other hand is not dependent on your circumstances.

That is good news! Jesus told the disciples he would be going away and that they would grieve. This situation was a significant happening in their lives. Jesus also told them that the Spirit of Truth, Counselor, or Holy Spirit would come and give them joy that no one could take away. The spiritual joy Jesus promises believers is rooted in a power much more potent than the conditions and happenings in life. Joy is one of the fruits of the Holy Spirit (Galatians 5:22 NIV).

No doubt, circumstances can make life challenging, and following Christ does not make you immune to sadness. Focusing on the trial of the moment is both easy and human. Yet the events of today are fleeting compared to the deep-seated joy that comes with knowing God is bigger than your biggest problems and that he loves you and will be with you forever and ever.

Healthy Laughter

In addition to the joy of the Holy Spirit, God has designed us so that joy, a cheerful heart, and laughter all do us good. Healthy laughter can do a lot to lift the human spirit. When he promises those who weep now that they will laugh, Jesus is confirming the value of laughter (Luke 6:21 NIV).

"A cheerful heart is good medicine," says Proverbs 17:22 NIV. God designed our bodies so that they actually respond in a healthy way when we laugh. Researchers at the University of Maryland, School of Medicine, have shown that when people laugh, their blood vessels expand and work better. The resulting increased blood flow has many health benefits. Laughter really is good medicine.[2]

An Intermission of Humor

Give yourself a break from the issues of divorce. Find time each day to seek the joy and peace of the Lord. Find

114

the humor in creation, in situations, or in entertainment. Look for reasons to laugh aloud. Laughter is a God-given gift and excellent stress reliever.

Making Information and Ideas Work

1. How is the joy of the Holy Spirit different from happiness?

2. What does this mean to you as you cope with divorce-related circumstances?

3. What does it mean to you to know that the Holy Spirit offers a joy no one can take away?

4. How does a sense of humor help you when you face tensions related to divorce?

5. In what ways can you increase your opportunities for healthy, hardy laughter?

Talk with God--Ponder this reading and share your thoughts with God. Listen so that the Holy Spirit might fill you with wisdom and peace. What concrete actions do you need to take based on what God is saying to you?

Highlights from Chapter 4
Look Inside

1. Knowing yourself allows you to build on your strengths and grow in areas that need growth.

2. If worry, anxiety, and fear override faith, suffering increases.

3. By stepping back from fears and assessing their realities, you can get a grip on the truth of situations and then act to control risks.

4. Fear sees danger in the unknown. Allowing a fear to live in you will lead to worry, anxiety, discouragement, and timidity.

5. Faith in God sees possibilities in the unknown. Choosing faith allows God to strengthen you and hold you up victorious.

6. Faith in God gives power, love, self-discipline, and encouragement. A faith-filled spirit empowers you.

7. Scripture gives a three-step guide to living in faith rather than in fear. 1) Remember that the Lord is near. 2) Replace anxiety by talking with God about everything. 3) With a thankful heart, tell God your needs. God will guard your heart and mind in Christ Jesus and give you peace.

8. You will still have to cope with the natural consequences of your choices, but God will forgive you if you sincerely ask. God doesn't forgive you because you are good—he forgives you because he is good.

9. Forgive yourself and ask God what he would have you learn from your mistakes.

10. Six steps for dealing with guilt and regrets are as follows: acknowledge regrets and guilt to God; change what you can;

accept what is now beyond your control; release regrets and guilt to God; ask God what he wants you to learn from your experiences; and allow yourself to learn and grow.

11. Different influences can go into someone's decision to leave a marriage. Not all of them have to do with the merits of the individual left.

12. Recovering from divorce includes working through grief.

13. Feeling very down, over the losses that come with divorce is normal.

14. Shifts in your support network are likely to occur and may create a sense of living in Limbo Land. Use this time to move away from the past and toward establishing your new life as an independent person.

15. Learning to be comfortable by yourself is empowering.

16. As you establish your support network, find people who will help you grow. Avoid people who bring you down.

17. Fulfilling the desire of human love will be much more within your reach if you first allow the perfect and unfailing love of God to heal you and empower you.

18. Do a readiness reality check before beginning a romance.

19. Joy is possible even when life's circumstances don't make you happy.

20. Find reasons to laugh – take a break from the issues of divorce.

CHAPTER 5

CAST AWAY STONES

The desire to blame and hurt the other person can derail you from your personal goal of finding peace after divorce.

Anger and hurt may lead to a desire to hurl stones at the person who has done you wrong. Harsh feelings toward your former spouse may result in revenge, blame, and hostility. Anger has its place, but prolonged anger is an internal acid that hurts you more than it hurts the other person. Living with a victim mindset steals your power because focusing on how you've been done wrong keeps you from taking charge of your own life. Casting away stones requires working through hostility related areas and letting go of their negative influences in your life.

Anger with God versus Reliance on God

*Create in me a pure heart, O God, and
renew a steadfast spirit within me. Do not cast me from
your presence or take your Holy Spirit from me.
Restore to me the joy of your salvation and grant me a
willing spirit, to sustain me.*

Psalms 51:10-12 NIV

"I hope this doesn't come off wrong, but sometimes I get really angry with God," says Jay. "I'm angry that he let me end up divorced--twice. I'm angry that he doesn't fix it all. Isn't he even listening to me?"

If you are angry with God, tell him so. The Bible has many stories of people who at times feel that God is distant and who exclaim their frustrations to God. "Even when I call out or cry for help, he shuts out my prayer," says the Bible in Lamentations 3:8.

Sometimes we get mad at God because we tend to believe that if God loves us, he will make everything work out the way we want. There are two problems with that line of thought. First, it ignores the truth that we must live with the consequences of our choices and often the consequences of the choices of others. Second, it assumes that we know more than God does. God does not cause divorce, people do. God does specialize in renewal.

120

A Bigger Vision

Because God is God and we are not, his vision is ever so much bigger. He does not cause divorce, but his ability to use the associated trials for good far exceeds our limited vision. In a state of divorce despair, I would never have envisioned that God would find any good use for the pain and anxiety I felt. That he would someday use it to help others going through divorce was beyond my comprehension.

The same person who wrote words of frustration in Lamentations 3:8 goes on after reflection to say, "Because of the Lord's great love we are not consumed, for his compassions never fail" (Lamentations 3:22). Crying out in frustration to God opens the lines of communication with your creator--the one who is most able to help you heal.

Where Are You God?

Even if you are not angry with God, he may seem like he is just not around. Rest assured, he is very much with you. The Holy Spirit often speaks to us as he did to Elijah in 1 Kings – In "a still small voice." Quiet your mind and heart and listen to God. He promises that he is "with you always, to the very end of the age" (Matthew 28:20).

God is big. He is the greatest source of compassion ever conceived. He is the author of hope and healing. God loves you even when you find yourself un-loveable. Seek him for he can create a steadfast spirit in you and restore you to joy. Divorce hurts, but prolonged anger toward God is misdirected. God is not the source of the darkness. God lifts the darkness.

The truth is that staying angry at God puts distance between you and the greatest resource for comfort and strength. Stumbling through the fallout of divorce by your-self because you remain angry with God is exceedingly lonely. Relying on God opens the door for him to heal your spirit and guide you to a better life.

Making Information and Ideas Work

1. If you are angry with God, what are the specifics of your anger?

2. How does this anger keep you in darkness?

3. You have the power to choose to be angry with God or to rely on God. What is your choice?

Talk with God--Ponder this reading and share your thoughts with God. Listen so that the Holy Spirit might fill you with wisdom and peace. What concrete actions do you need to take based on what God is saying to you?

Stuck in a State of Done Wrong

Turn to me and be gracious to me,
for I am lonely and afflicted.
The troubles of my heart have multiplied;
free me from my anguish.

Psalm 25:16-17 NIV

Initially, it can be easy to stew in thoughts and feelings about how you've been done wrong. A reasonable amount of stewing may actually help you emotionally let go of the other person. Yet, continuing to dwell on how you've been done wrong will tie you to the past, rather than propel you into a positive future. It is a miserable way to live.

Most people I've met who are stuck in a state of Done Wrong are flabbergasted by the injustice of their former spouse's choices. They tend to see themselves as good mates, which further fuels the fire about unfairness. Some focus continued energies on being ditched unfairly. Others refuse to let go of resentment that the behavior of their mate caused them to be so frustrated with their marriage that they had to be the one to leave.

If you find yourself stuck in Done Wrong, here are a few things to consider:

- As hard as it is to accept, the other person's choices may not be completely about you. People make

123

choices based on a variety of influences from both their past and current experiences.

- While you may be a conscientious spouse, what you gave to the relationship may not have been what your former spouse expected or needed.
- The frustration and disillusionment you feel are understandable, yet being stuck in a state of Done Wrong is a barrier to finding peace after divorce.

Anger and feeling wounded over the choices of your former mate can lead to a victim mentality. Assuming the role of a victim is a dead end. Even if you were treated unfairly, assuming a victim mentality focuses you on the past and steals your power to move beyond the hurt. Living in 'done wrong' is like throwing a boomerang. The resentment and anger are aimed at your former spouse, but the real receiver of grief ends up being you.

Stuck in a perpetual state of Done Wrong casts you into a downward spiral and feeds your mistrust of others. It is important to acknowledge feelings of Done Wrong and to process them. Yet, living in them for a long time is futile.

When you dwell in Done Wrong, you feed your own anguish. Decide to let go of 'done wrong' thoughts every time they surface and say--I will not feed my own anguish. If you find you are unable to resolve feeling done wrong on your own, seek professional counseling.

Get rid of all bitterness, rage and anger, brawling and slander, along with every form of malice.

Ephesians 4:31 NIV

Making Information and Ideas Work

1. How do the key points in this section on *Stuck in a State of Done Wrong* relate to your life?

Talk with God--Ponder this reading and share your thoughts with God. Listen so that the Holy Spirit might fill you with wisdom and peace. What concrete actions do you need to take based on what God is saying to you?

Revenge

Never pay back evil with more evil.
Do things in such a way that everyone can see you are
honorable. Do all that you can to live in peace with
everyone. Dear friends, never take revenge. Leave that to
the righteous anger of God.... Don't let evil conquer you,
but conquer evil by doing good.

Romans 12:17-19, 21 NLT

The Sweet Taste

Deep hurts, dished out by someone we have loved, can leave us burnt and sizzling inside. We may feel like the only way to sooth this seething resentment is with payback--an eye for an eye, a hurt for a hurt. Revenge can range from making biting comments and withholding cooperation, to damaging property and acting violently. Getting even with those who have done us wrong may give us the feeling that we have corrected an injustice. Even contemplating revenge can feel good.

Anger's Outlet

Revenge is an unhealthy outlet for anger. Anger needs to be recognized, expressed, and healed, but revenge is not a healthy solution. Revenge turns anger into the conscious attempt to hurt another person and is inconsistent with the way Christ taught us to treat each other.

The True Costs of Revenge

Revenge may taste sweet at the time, but the behavior of revenge can end up being a source of regret and embarrassment in the end. The internal consequences are insidious. They creep into your soul and eat a hole in your relationship with God. Below are four prices you can pay for revenge.

Self-Destruction

By fueling anger with hateful thoughts and resentful feelings, we feed our unhappiness. Despite the temporary high it brings, revenge is like pouring acid on our own souls. In an effort to punish another person, we heap burning coals on our psyches, distance ourselves from God, and hinder finding peace after divorce. An eye-for-an-eye philosophy is contrary to the spirit of Christ. "Do not answer a fool according to his folly, or you will be like him yourself" (Proverbs 26:4). You can choose to seek payback or choose to heal. Being vindictive will hinder healing.

Loss of Victory

Revenge is yielding power, not claiming victory. When we choose revenge, we allow the other person's bad behavior to determine our behavior. We are making a choice to act like the other person rather than making a deliberate choice to rely on the strength of God to help us rise above the actions of another human being. "Do not repay evil with evil or insult with insult, but with blessing, because to this you were called so that you may inherit a blessing" (1 Peter 3:9).

Loss of Energy and Peace

Revenge zaps your strength and steals your peace. It robs you of energy you need to move forward with your life. An I'll-get-you-back attitude perpetuates a cycle of hostility. When the dust settles, you may end up feeling rather foolish knowing you put a lot of energy into revenge that you could have been putting into your own healing. Feeding hostility does not make any situation better. It is especially tragic when children are directly or indirectly victims of such negativity between their parents.

We are distracted from God's plan for our lives when we focus our energies on getting back at our former spouses. The hatred that inspires revenge is not of God. It is instead, a wall we put up that separates us from his peace. "My dear brothers, take note of this: Everyone should be quick to listen, slow to speak and slow to become angry, for man's anger does not bring about the righteous life that God desires" (James 1:19-20).

Compromised Future Relationships

Revenge toward a former spouse is a huge detriment for future relationships. Feelings of revenge are energy suckers that take away from the ability to build quality in a new relationship. Worse yet, marrying someone to get back at a former spouse may suggest stronger feelings for the former spouse than for the new mate. "Do not say, 'I'll pay you back for this wrong!' Wait for the LORD, and he will deliver you" (Proverbs 20:22).

If Not Revenge, Then What?

It is unlikely that you can just switch off feelings of revenge. Letting go of profound hurt and anger does not happen instantly just because you decide not to seek revenge. Nonetheless, there are strategies that can help you head off any vengeful actions and move beyond the desire for revenge. *Anger toward Your Former Spouse*, the next reading in this book, offers some thoughts on dealing with anger.

The Pay-Off of Choosing the Higher Ground

Choosing higher ground rather than wading in the muck of revenge has wonderful pay-off. Seeking God rather than revenge is healing. By turning to Christ, we are empowered to live by the Holy Spirit and to find peace rather than the turmoil associated with revenge.

128

"So I say, live by the Spirit, and you will not gratify the desires of the sinful nature," (Galatians 5:16). Galatians also tells us that, "the fruit of the Spirit is love, joy, peace, patience, kindness, goodness, faithfulness, gentleness and self-control" (Galatians 5:22-23). That surely beats any satisfaction gained through revenge.

Making Information and Ideas Work for You

1. Why is the temptation to seek revenge so attractive?

2. Despite its appeal, in what ways is revenge self-destructive?

3. How is choosing revenge yielding power to the person with whom you are angry?

4. How does focusing energy on revenge put a barrier between God's peace and you?

5. What choices are you making about how to deal with anger and resentment toward your former spouse?

6. What choices can you make to help yourself shed the desire for revenge and to move closer to living a life filled with the fruit of the Holy Spirit?

Talk with God--Ponder this reading and share your thoughts with God. Listen so that the Holy Spirit might fill you with wisdom and peace. What concrete actions do you need to take based on what God is saying to you?

'In your anger do not sin:'
Do not let the sun go down while you are
still angry, and do not give
the devil a foothold.

Ephesians 4:26-27 NIV

Anger toward Your Former Spouse

A fool gives full vent to his anger,
but a wise man keeps himself under control.

Proverbs 29:11 NIV

Many of our divorce workshop participants have reported being amazed at the intensity of their divorce-related anger. Such anger may lead people to act in ways that are totally outside of how they normally behave. The above scripture from Proverbs acknowledges that feeling anger is a normal part of being human. It also implies that even though feeling anger may be normal, what we do with that anger makes all of the difference.

Your choices will determine whether any anger you feel results in positive or negative outcomes. Here are some things to consider as you process divorce-related anger and work to A.R.R.I.V.E. at a more peaceful place.

- **A**dmit that you are angry.
- **R**ecognize that you have a choice in how to deal with your anger.
- **R**ealistically assess your anger.
- **I**dentify appropriate actions.
- **V**ent emotions appropriately.
- **E**merge from holding yourself a prisoner of anger.

Admit That You are Angry

Some people find it hard to admit that they are angry. They deny their anger and cloak the emotion with softer phrases like "I'm hurt." You cannot resolve your anger unless you first identify it and call it what it is.

At the other end of the spectrum are people who sizzle and burn with rage, often exploding in inappropriate ways. Getting the anger out has value, but the spin-off can do more damage than good if the expression of anger is inappropriate.

Recognize That You Have a Choice

When feelings of anger arise, you have a choice of how to deal with them. Realizing this can empower you to stop before you act and to consider your actions and the consequences of your actions. Knowing you have a choice allows you to act in a way that increases your chances for the best outcomes.

Realistically Assess Your Anger

Exactly why are you angry? What thoughts fuel your anger? Is your anger productive or counterproductive? Is anger keeping you from moving forward with your life?

Identify Constructive Actions

Stewing in anger is counterproductive, but sometimes appropriately expressed anger serves a purpose. Jesus expressed anger when he entered the temple and drove out those who were selling animals for sacrifice, and those who where exchanging other monies for official Jewish currency.

These people, including priests, were making a profit at the expense of the poor in the name of worshiping God. Jesus' anger and action was justified because as he said, "The Scriptures declare, 'My Temple will be called a house of prayer,' but you have turned it into a den of thieves!" (Matthew 21:13, NLT).

Healthy anger helps put issues into perspective and can help direct positive action that is in keeping with the will of God. Healthy anger can motivate a parent to take the actions needed to protect children from an abusive spouse. A healthy degree of anger can help break unhealthy emotional ties, or stir determination not to let the behavior of your former spouse lower your self-esteem.

Allow anger to motivate positive action that is in keeping with a Christian spirit. Cussing out your former spouse or keying that person's car paint are not appropriate ways to express anger. Often the most productive way to deal with anger does not happen in the interactions with your former spouse. Instead, it happens inside of yourself as you find appropriate ways to vent anger and work to let it go.

Vent Emotions Appropriately

Express your anger in a way that allows you to blow off steam without creating any negative consequences for yourself or others. One man says he is able to release pent up anger by chopping firewood. Others cite the value of talking with a sympathetic friend. It is much better to state to a friend that you are angry with your former spouse, or to jog or take a brisk walk, than to blow up at your children or lose your cool at work. Such misdirected anger unjustly hurts those you love and may have negative outcomes for you.

The directive not to let the sun go down on our anger reflects the detrimental impact of holding on to anger (Ephesians 4:26-27). For our own good and our ability to serve God, we need to let go of anger as soon as possible. Letting go of anger is not the same as continuing to subject yourself to poor treatment.

Emerge from Your Own Prison

Anger may be justified and serve a purpose, but the choice to continue to live in anger can be a form of self-imprisonment. Choosing to live angry is choosing to be miserable. Consuming anger does not harm the other person but instead gives that person emotional control in your life.

Make a conscious decision to identify and appropriately vent your anger, then work toward letting go of that anger. Be patient with yourself. It can take repeated daily effort, time, and prayer to work through anger. If your anger is so powerful that you have trouble working through it on your own, seek professional help.

Making Information and Ideas Work

1. List specific things about your former spouse, separation, or divorce that most stir your anger.

2. What choices can you make about how to deal with that anger?

3. How can you get your anger out without creating negative consequences for yourself or others?

Talk with God--Ponder this reading and share your thoughts with God. Listen so that the Holy Spirit might fill you with wisdom and peace. What concrete actions do you need to take based on what God is saying to you?

Blame

Do not seek revenge or bear a grudge
against one of your people, but love your
neighbor as yourself. I am the LORD.

Leviticus 19:18 NIV

"This is his fault," says Judy. "If only he had not…"

When a relationship has enough bumps and bruises that at least one party decides the marriage is over, there can be plenty of reasons to point a finger. If we can place the blame somewhere, then maybe we can make the whole situation somehow make sense. Blame is anger turned outward. (If you are blaming yourself, see the section on guilt.)

Blame may stem from things that were done, or things that were not done. Perhaps your former mate has said or done hurtful things or failed to provide the needed support. Blame may also reflect things you think your former mate should have done differently such as parent or manage money differently.

The problem with blame is that no good future comes from it. Blame does not solve any problems. Even when justified, blame has a negative backlash for the person who does the blaming. Blame can lead to grudges and revenge. Grudges and revenge reduce your ability to accept God's gifts of love and peace.

Blaming may also be a way to sidestep personal responsibility. If grief is all someone else's fault, then we assume no responsibility for problems with the marriage. Sadly, if we assume no responsibility for our faults, it will be difficult to assume responsibility for our growth.

Removing blame from your thoughts can take effort and prayer, but it is possible. The first step is to identify the hurts that lead you to blame. Take your time as you answer the questions that follow. Write what comes to mind now and add to your answers as you ponder the questions over the next week.

Making Information and Ideas Work

1. To stimulate your thoughts, look back at your timeline
    in Chapter 2 at the end of the section on *Moving from
    Acceptance to Renewal.* Make a list of things you wish
    your former or soon to be former spouse had done dif-
    ferently.

2. Do the things you have written down include all of the
    things for which you blame your former spouse? If not,
    add to the list.

3. How can you apply the content of the section on *Blame*
    to each item you have listed in numbers 1 and 2 in this
    section?

Talk with God--Ponder this reading and share your
thoughts with God. Listen so that the Holy Spirit might fill
you with wisdom and peace. What concrete actions do you
need to take based on what God is saying to you?

Forgiving Your Former Spouse

Forgive us our sins, for we also forgive everyone who sins against us. And lead us not into temptation.

Luke 11:4 NIV

Why Forgive?

Refusing to forgive is like refusing to eat in order to starve the un-forgiven person. It does not work. Forgiveness is not about the other person but is instead about your relationship with yourself and with God. Dwelling in un-forgiveness corrodes your spirit with resentment and bitterness. Experiencing forgiving in your heart is important to renewing yourself. Forgiveness enables you to let go.

Un-forgiveness clouds your vision with resentment and hate. Forgiveness clears your vision so that you can move forward. When you forgive, it is for your own good, not because the other person deserves it.

The Reality about Forgiveness

Forgiveness does not make offensive behavior forgettable nor does it make it acceptable. Forgiveness will not take away the memory of bad behavior. What it does take away is the sting, anger, and bitterness that reside in you when you hold a grudge. Forgiveness is not the same as reconciliation with the person who committed the wrong. In fact, that person may or may not know about your forgiveness, and may or may not care.

Forgiveness is not an emotion; it is an assortment of choices. It is a choice to let go of blame, resentment, and the need for revenge. It is a choice instead to nurture your heart with positive things. It is a choice to let the behavior of the person you blame quit controlling your emotions and thoughts. "Above all else, guard your heart, for it is the wellspring of life" (Proverbs 4:23). Forgiveness is a choice to protect your heart and grow closer to the blessings and peace of God.

God, Help Me to Want to Forgive

If ever the idiom, "It's easier said than done," fit anything, it is the action of forgiveness. Forgiving is not a simple act. Forgiving is an important journey of the mind and heart. In fact, it is a battle within the mind that you may have to fight everyday for a long time.

For a while during separation, and even after divorce, not forgiving may feel good. It may feel justified and right to stoke the fires of anger that keep un-forgiveness blazing. Total forgiveness takes determination and prayer, as well as a conscious choice to heal your soul and spirit.

Steps in Forgiving

"Before the Lord walked me through this journey, I thought 'forgiving' somebody was pretty lame," says Roberta Grace when speaking of her own healing from divorce. "I thought it was about forgetting what had happened. And it didn't work either."

Roberta struggled to cope after her "life crash" when her marriage dissolved. Turning to God, Roberta learned the deep meaning of Christian forgiveness. She stresses the daily commitment that forgiveness requires as she says, "Satan still throws me a fishing hook sometimes, just to see if I will bite at the bait. No way."

Roberta explains, "Forgiveness means reworking the old patterns of thought in your mind until the truth of Jesus becomes your new pattern." The following are Roberta's steps to total forgiveness[3].

Grace's Steps to Total Forgiveness
Used with Permission – Roberta Grace 2008

1. *I forgive you. I had to repeat this over and over until my teeth unclenched, and I really meant it.*

2. *I forgive you for_____. I had to list all those things for which I forgave him. Sometimes I would think of new things.*

3. *I forgive you and I pray for you. The Lord says pray for those who do you wrong.*

4. *I forgive you and ask the Lord to bless you. I had to repeat this until my teeth unclenched and I meant it. I prayed that he receive all those good things in life that I also wanted such as: peace, happiness, love, prosperity, safety, good relationships, and Jesus in his life. I still pray this one, over and over.*

5. I forgive you and I will not keep a record of your wrongdoings. *I had to cast all those wrongs into the sea or at the foot of Jesus every time they came up, and commit to not reviewing them and not speaking about them but only saying good things. The power of life and death are in the tongue.*

6. I will totally forgive you even if it takes the rest of my life. *I will forgive, as I have been forgiven by God. I am committed to forgiving again, again, and again, until Satan gives up at tempting me.*

Making Ideas and Information Work

1. List the wrongs you have suffered from your former spouse. You may find it helpful to review your answers to the questions on blame in the last section of this book.

2. After reflecting on what you just wrote, re-read Roberta's list and ask God to strengthen you as you work to clear your heart of the grief of un-forgiveness.

Talk with God--Ponder this reading and share your thoughts with God. Listen so that the Holy Spirit might fill you with wisdom and peace. What concrete actions do you need to take based on what God is saying to you?

Highlights from Chapter 5
Cast Away Stones

1. Staying angry at God puts distance between you and the greatest source of comfort and strength you can know.

2. Living your life dwelling on having been done wrong will tie you to the past rather than propel you into a positive future.

3. The desire to blame and hurt the other person can derail you from finding peace after divorce.

4. Grudges and revenge reduce your ability to accept God's gifts of love and peace.

5. Earnestly praying for your former spouse does not make that person right, but it does open your heart to peace.

6. What you do with that anger makes a big difference in whether the anger you feel results in positive or negative outcomes regarding your ability to recover from divorce.

7. A.R.R.I.V.E is a formula for coping with the anger of divorce. (See section on anger.)

8. Forgiveness is not about the other person but is instead about your relationship with yourself and with God. When you forgive, it is for your own good, not because the other person deserves it.

9. Forgiveness is a choice. Forgiveness is not the same as reconciliation with the person who committed the wrong. Total forgiveness may take concentrated effort and time.

CHAPTER 6

REDIRECT YOUR THOUGHTS

Thoughts and beliefs can set you up for success or seriously hinder your progress.

"For as he thinks in his heart, so is he," says Proverbs 23:7 (NKJV). Thoughts hold great power in determining how you process your experiences and how you choose to react to the things that are happening in your life. Thoughts impact how you feel, what you believe, and what you do.

Your thoughts are central to how you deal with divorce. Thoughts can set you up for success or seriously hinder your ability to move past divorce in a positive way. Chapter 6 revisits some of the issues previously discussed and shows how replacing unhealthy thoughts with healthy thoughts can greatly improve your ability to learn from your divorce, and to live a joyful and peaceful life.

The Power in Thoughts

I have come into the world as a light,
so that no one who believes in me should stay in darkness.

John 12:46 NIV

"I'm doomed to live a lonely life," says Janie. "I always feel so very lonesome."

"Living alone isn't what I wanted, but I'm adjusting," responds James. "I'm making new friends and finding new things to do. I'm by myself, but I don't see any reason I have to feel lonely all the time. Besides, I know God is always with me."

Each of the above comments illustrates how thoughts can influence your outcomes. Thinking you are doomed to live a lonely life will likely leave you feeling lonely. Continuing to accept a feeling of doomed loneliness will result in decisions that keep you feeling lonely for a long time. On the other hand, deciding to fill the loneliness with friends and the presence of God keeps being alone from always being lonely. For Janie and James, the difference in outcomes is rooted in the difference in their thinking.

Thoughts can support finding peace after divorce or can prevent it. What you think colors who you are, how you feel, how you act, and what you believe. Thoughts are powerful since they create your mindset. God has given you

144

the ability either to choose thoughts that keep you in darkness, or to choose thoughts that allow you to live in the light that is a gift of Christ.

Darkness Thoughts

These self-defeating thoughts are barriers that take away personal power and leave a victim mindset. They are thoughts that are distant from the promises and Spirit of God. Repeated, Darkness Thoughts lead to self-defeating behaviors that prevent moving past the fall-out of divorce. Yet, Jesus promises that no one who believes in him must remain in darkness. Darkness Thoughts are powerless when replaced with thoughts brightened by the light of Christ.

In-the-Light Thoughts

In-the-Light Thoughts feed an awareness of God's promise of a future and a hope (Jeremiah 29:11). Thoughts that create an empowering mindset and inspire healthy growth are In-the-light Thoughts. Even when circumstances are not great, In-the-Light Thoughts support making choices that will have the most positive outcomes. In-the-Light Thoughts encourage learning from mistakes. They draw minds closer to God and lead to the healing, joy, and peace that are consistent with the promises of God. Because In-the-Light Thoughts are in line with God, they always have the power to conquer Darkness Thoughts.

The Value of Thinking about Thoughts

Thought patterns are ways of thinking that have developed into habits. When Darkness Thoughts become habits, they sabotage healing, growth, and peace. Thinking about

145

thoughts allows you to identify and replace those that hold you back. Just because a thought occurs does not mean you must accept it.

Changing a thought pattern takes intent, effort, and prayer. Below are some questions to consider when thinking about your thoughts.

- What is my goal?
- Is this thought helping me move toward my goal, or is it blocking my ability to reach my goal?
- Is this thought consistent with Jesus' love and the word of God?
- If it is a Darkness Thought, then what healthier In-the-Light Thought can I choose to replace it?
- How can I remind myself to practice the new In-the-Light Thought?

Claiming a New Way of Thinking

Talking to God supports identifying In-the-Light Thoughts and claiming them. Knowing God's promises as stated in the Bible can help you to recognize thoughts consistent with the hope offered by Christ. Once you recognize a Darkness Thought and identify an In-the-Light Thought to replace it, repeat the new thought as many times as needed until it replaces the Darkness Thought. With practice, determination, and prayer, you can replace self-defeating thoughts. Since thoughts tie to emotions and to behavior, shifting to In-the-Light Thoughts can help you to feel better and to make better choices.

How much practice it will take to replace a Darkness Thought with an In-the-Light Thought depends on how entrenched the Darkness Thought has become. Since Jesus came into the world as a light, it only makes sense that if you seek him, the Holy Spirit will help you in your efforts to move out of the darkness. In fact, that is the promise of John 12:46.

The Darkness/In-the-Light Thought Principle

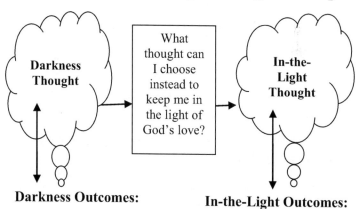

Darkness Outcomes:

- Self-defeating behavior

In-the-Light Outcomes:

- Positive behavior that supports a hope and future

A New Perspective

Redirecting thoughts in a positive way creates a healing perspective on life. When seeking peace after divorce, four main areas merit consideration:

- Thoughts about God
- Thoughts about marriage and divorce
- Thoughts about circumstances
- Thoughts about your former spouse

The next sections of this chapter provide the opportunity to explore each of these areas.

Making Information and Ideas Work

Think of a troublesome thought regarding your divorce and then answer the following questions:

1. Does this thought help me move toward my goal of healing from divorce and finding peace? If not, how is this thought blocking my ability to reach my goal?

2. Is this thought consistent with Jesus' love and the word of God? Why or why not?

3. If this is a Darkness Thought, what In-the-Light Thought will I choose to replace it?

Talk with God--Ponder this reading and share your thoughts with God. Listen so that the Holy Spirit might fill you with wisdom and peace. What concrete actions do you need to take based on what God is saying to you?

Thoughts and Beliefs about God

For God so loved the world that he gave his one and only Son, that whoever believes in him shall not perish but have eternal life.

John 3:16 NIV

Beliefs are thoughts the mind accepts with confidence as truths. Yet unlike cold facts, beliefs are likely to have a spiritual or emotional aspect. Thoughts build beliefs, reflect beliefs, and reinforce beliefs. Beliefs develop from experiences, relationships, and choices, providing a framework for thoughts, emotions, and actions.

An Open Door or a Closed Door?

Beliefs about God, and the thoughts that go with them, have an impact on the ability to recover from divorce with God's help. Thoughts either open or close the door to God's healing power. Your receptiveness determines whether you feel God's presence and help. The Bible tells us, "Look! I stand at the door and knock. If you hear my voice and open the door, I will come in, and we will share a meal together as friends" (Revelation 3:20, NLT).

Does God See Me as Worthy of His Support?

Rejection associated with divorce and a sense of personal failure may leave you thinking yourself unworthy to receive

149

God's love and forgiveness. The Darkness Thought that God sees you as unfit or is angry with you will likely cause you to distance yourself from God or to try to earn your way back into his favor. Neither action will move you forward. Ignoring God leaves you empty. Trying to be perfect leaves you frustrated. Such Darkness Thoughts may end up keeping you from talking to God at all.

If you fail to seek God, you will miss all of his promises. Refuse to accept Darkness Thoughts. Instead, focus on the In-the-Light Thought that God loves you because he is good and merciful, not because you are perfect. "So if the Son sets you free, you will be free indeed" (John 8:36). You can then know the fruits of his Spirit which are, "love, joy, peace, patience, kindness, goodness, faithfulness, gentleness and self-control" (from Galatians 5:22-23).

Indifferent or Caring?

If you think of God as an old man sitting on a throne, he may seem like someone who is distant and not interested in your daily struggles. However if you replace that thought with the understanding that God is caring and wants you to walk with him daily, you will draw closer to God and find that, "I can do everything through him (God) who gives me strength" (Philippians 4:13). The belief that faith in God means you should have no problems, or the belief that God has caused your problems, will leave you frustrated with God. The truth is that while it seems to defy logic, you can have peace in God even when you are suffering. You can trust that God uses the trials of life to make you a stronger person of perseverance, character, and hope (Romans 5:1-

4). This is often easier to see in hindsight than it is in the midst of our trials.

The children's song, "Jesus Loves Me" points out that we can know that Jesus loves us "because the Bible tells me so." Indeed, the scriptures speak of the love of God and therefore can be helpful in finding In-the-Light Thoughts about God. Points of hope from the Bible can be helpful tools for fending off Darkness Thoughts. They may be scripture quotes or simple phrases like, "God loves me and has a plan for me," or, "I can get through this with God's help." Repeat your favorite scriptures and phrases as often as needed until Darkness Thoughts are replaced with In-the-Light Thoughts.

The Power of Praise

Praising God has incredible healing power, even when praising seems like an unlikely thing to do. Lifting praises to the Lord supports an In-the-Light mindset and tunes our thoughts to the amazing power of God. "Give thanks to the LORD, for he is good; his love endures forever" (Psalm 118:1).

---

*Set your minds on things above,
not on earthly things.*

Colossians 3:2 NIV

The Darkness/In-the-Light Thought Principle: Example of a Thought about God

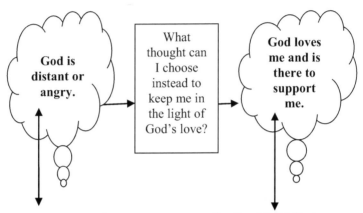

Darkness Outcomes:
- I don't talk with God.
- I must cope with divorce without Devine help.
- The future seems hopeless.
- My heart grows cold and more afraid or angry.

In-the-Light Outcomes:
- I am worthwhile.
- God strengthens me.
- God has a plan for me.
- My spirits are uplifted.

Making Information and Ideas Work

1. Do you feel you are thinking about God in a way that helps you deal positively with your divorce? Explain.

2. What Darkness Thoughts do you have that keep you from feeling God's supportive love or fully developing a healing relationship with him?

   Example Darkness Thought: I cannot have God's peace because my marriage fell apart.

3. What In-the-Light Thoughts can you use to replace these Darkness Thoughts?

   Example In-the-Light Thought: The good news is that I can still have peace through Jesus Christ.

4. What scripture can you use to support your new In-the-Light Thoughts?

   Example of Supportive Scripture: "You know the message God sent to the people of Israel, telling the good news of peace through Jesus Christ, who is Lord of all." Acts 10:36

Talk with God--Ponder this reading and share your thoughts with God. Listen so that the Holy Spirit might fill you with wisdom and peace. What concrete actions do you need to take based on what God is saying to you?

Thoughts about Marriage and Divorce

I can do everything through him who gives me strength.

Philippians 4:13 NIV

It is an understatement to say that divorce brings stressful times. Your thoughts on marriage, divorce, and the singleness that results from divorce affect your ability to get through those times successfully and to thrive after divorce. Below are some examples.

Thoughts about Marriage

The idea that one person alone can make a marriage work, even though the other person has clearly signed off on the marriage, is a Darkness Thought. It places unnecessarily guilt on a mate who has made every effort to save the marriage. Understanding that saving a marriage takes effort on the part of both partners lifts a self-imposed burden of total responsibility. The replacement In-the-Light Thought acknowledges that one person cannot make the other person want to stay in a marriage.

Thoughts about Divorce

Darkness Thoughts, such as believing divorce represents the end of all happiness, block the ability to find happiness. Such thoughts create a self-fulfilling prophecy since you tend to become what you think you will be--unhappy. On the other hand, you increase your ability to be joyful if you think that finding joy in God is possible even though you are unhappy about divorce.

Thoughts about Singleness after Divorce

Thoughts about singleness influence reactions to being single. Thinking that single people need a mate to make them whole is a Darkness Thought that may result in seeking a mate before working through the fallout of divorce. It may also prevent learning to be whole as an individual fulfilled by a relationship with Christ.

The In-the-Light Thought to replace this Darkness Thought is that you can be whole without having a mate because only God can make you whole. Knowing you can be whole with God frees you to stay single or decide to seek another mate once you've recovered from your divorce. If you are looking to God rather than to another human for your sense of wholeness, you are actually a better candidate for a successful marriage should you decide to marry again.

If you believe that singleness is necessarily lonely, you will be lonely. If you believe you can be unmarried and not be lonely, you will grow to enjoy your own space and develop an interesting life with friends, hobbies, and social activities. Your thoughts about singleness will set the tone for your success in adjusting to life as a single person.

Thoughts about Single Parenting

Many myths exist about single parenting and it can be easy to buy into them. If you believe that children whose parents are divorced can't be well adjusted, you may add much anxiety to your life and your children's lives. If you know that children of divorce can be well adjusted with the proper support and love, you can work to make that happen. If you think you are unable to be a good parent on your own, you will feed self-doubt. If you think that you are still as good a parent as ever, you will be just that.

The Darkness/In-the-Light Thought Principle: Example of a Thought about Singleness

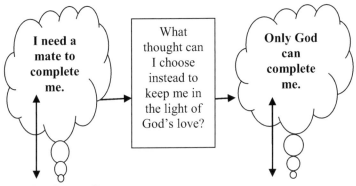

Darkness Outcomes:	In-the-Light Outcomes:
• I focus on finding a mate rather than healing.	• I focus on healing from divorce and becoming complete as an individual in relationship with God.
• Old problems carry over into new relationships.	
• I rely on a fallible human rather than the all powerful God for my sense of well-being.	• By focusing on healing and finding completion with God, I increase my contentment as an individual and increase my chance of a successful marriage if I should marry again.

How Can I Know if I Should Marry Again?

Many factors go into deciding if, and when, you should marry again. Obviously, finding the right person is paramount. Yet there are other considerations as well. Here are a few things to keep in mind.

Remember--Only God Can Complete You

Those looking to a mate to, "make me whole" will always be disappointed because their mate cannot be God. Seek to know God and receive his love before seeking a mate. Only a right relationship with God can complete you. Grow in him and he will reveal his will for your life and it will be good. Marriage can be a delightful partnership when two people are each seeking God for their fulfillment.

Fix What Needs to be Fixed

Focusing on finding a new marital partner to fill the void caused by divorce may result in another failed marriage unless the factors that contributed to divorce are addressed first. It is critical to take the initiative prayerfully to identify and address these issues and to seek counseling if needed.

Center Yourself

Joy and peace are available in a relationship with Christ. This means that a single person can live a joyous and full life. Delight in the wonders of creation and the presence of God.

Making Information and Ideas Work

1. What Darkness Thoughts do you have about marriage?

2. What In-the-Light Thoughts can replace them?

3. What Darkness Thoughts do you have about divorce?

4. What In-the-Light Thoughts do you need to replace them?

5. What Darkness Thoughts do you have about being single?

6. What In-the-Light Thoughts do you need to replace them?

Talk with God--Ponder this reading and share your thoughts with God. Listen so that the Holy Spirit might fill you with wisdom and peace. What concrete actions do you need to take based on what God is saying to you?

Brothers, I do not consider myself yet to have taken hold of it. But one thing I do: Forgetting what is behind and straining toward what is ahead, I press on toward the goal to win the prize for which God has called me heavenward in Christ Jesus.

Philippians 3:13-14 NIV

Thoughts about Circumstances

For we are God's masterpiece.
He has created us anew in Christ Jesus,
so we can do the good things he planned for us long ago.

Ephesians 2:10 NLT

What you tell yourself about circumstances is important to your ability to find peace after divorce. Thoughts that support your ability to tackle life's challenges and to influence your life for the good, place you on much better footing than thoughts that support powerlessness. Thoughts about circumstances are as important as the events of those circumstances.

Obstacles and Trials

Pursuing healing, peace, and a positive life after separation and divorce, includes coping with barriers along the way. Unexpected detours can cause setbacks, but they don't have to stop you cold. By approaching challenges with a mindset that says that you and God together can tackle anything, you are miles ahead of people who tell themselves that the struggle is just too hard.

"Everything goes wrong for me. I'll never be truly happy," represents the ultimate in Darkness Thoughts about circumstances. If you tell yourself that you are a victim and accept being a victim, Darkness Thoughts will keep you a victim. Yet if you ask yourself what you can learn from your experiences and then chart a course to make your life happen, your In-the-Light Thoughts will increase your chances of a positive new life.

Wallowing in problems is a sure way to saturate your life in self-pity. Thoughts that focus on the negative impact of divorce may become a life-long burden. Philippians 4:8 says, "Finally, brothers, whatever is true, whatever is noble, whatever is right, whatever is pure, whatever is lovely, whatever is admirable – if anything is excellent or praiseworthy – think about such things." Dwelling on the positive in itself will not change circumstances, but it will fortify you while you prayerfully work to improve your circumstances. Philippians 4:8 represents the ultimate in In-the-Light Thoughts about circumstances.

Hindsight or Vision

Moving forward after divorce means refocusing your thoughts from the past to the present and to the future. Hindsight is a type of Darkness Thinking that dwells on regrets. Focusing on regrets sucks you downward into the mire of the past. Such Darkness Thinking reinforces a feeling of failure.

In-the-Light Thinking tells you that the past does not have to predict your future. Circumstances related to your divorce do not change the fact that God created you to, "do the good things he planned for us (you) long ago" (Ephesians 2:10 NLT). Faith in God offers you a solid place to stand while shifting from thinking in hindsight to casting a vision for your future.

Emotional Responses to Circumstances

What you think about circumstances also affects your emotions. Thoughts that tell you to suppress emotions related to your circumstances force those emotions deep inside and keep them from being processed. In-the-Light Thoughts acknowledge that crying and appropriately venting anger can be part of the process of healing from divorce.

> *I know what it is to be in need, and I know what it is to have plenty. I have learned the secret of   being content in any and every situation,   whether well fed or hungry, whether living in plenty or in want. I can do everything through him who gives me strength.*
>
> Philippians 4:12-13 NIV

The Darkness/In-the-Light Principle: Example of a Thought about Circumstances

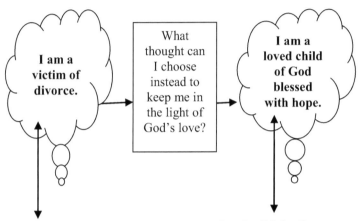

Darkness Outcomes:

- I feel stuck where I am.
- Things are out of my control.
- I've been done wrong and there is little that can be done about it.
- I remain a victim.

In-the-Light Outcomes:

- I decide to learn from the experience of divorce.
- I find ways to use the divorce experience to make my life better.
- I accept reality and take steps to make a new life for myself.
- I learn that the past does not have to dictate my future.
- I open myself to the joy of living in Christ.

Making Information and Ideas Work

1. Write one Darkness Thought you have regarding the obstacles and trials of your circumstances.

2. What In-the-Light Thought might you use to replace it?

3. If you are still living with thoughts rooted in the past, what In-the-Light Thoughts can help you refocus your thoughts to the present and future?

4. Do your thoughts allow you to express your emotions about the circumstances of your divorce? Explain.

Talk with God--Ponder this reading and share your thoughts with God. Listen so that the Holy Spirit might fill you with wisdom and peace. What concrete actions do you need to take based on what God is saying to you?

Thoughts about Your Former Spouse

Don't copy the behavior and customs of this world, but let God transform you into a new person by changing the way you think. Then you will learn to know God's will for you, which is good and pleasing and perfect.

Romans 12:2 NLT

Thoughts about your former spouse play a big role in your ability to break free of the past and move on with your life in a positive way. Redefining thoughts about your former spouse is a part of letting go of the past. Changing the nature of these thoughts may be particularly challenging due to strong emotional ties--both positive and negative. To move on with life, it is helpful to determine what thoughts about your former spouse need to change. By taking control of thoughts, you can also keep your former spouse from being able to continue to push your buttons. Here are some examples of how thoughts can perpetuate emotional ties or free you from the past.

Thinking and Emotional Ties

I will not forgive my former spouse because he does not deserve it, is a Darkness Thought. Concentrating on your former spouse's wrongdoings creates Darkness Thoughts. Thinking that you cannot forgive someone who does not deserve forgiveness keeps you trapped in the darkness of bitterness and resentment. In-the-Light Thoughts acknowledge that forgiveness is not about your former spouse. Forgiveness is about freeing yourself from the anger and negativity that a lack of forgiveness perpetuates in you. Forgiveness is a decision, not an emotion. I can forgive my former spouse without approving of the behavior I am forgiving, is an In-the-Light Thought.

Thinking that your former spouse should not have financial security greater than yours is a Darkness Thought if your property settlement has already been finalized by the courts. Your feelings may be justified, but holding this thought will not change reality. It will lead you to envy and frustration instead of peace.

Control and Responsibility

The idea that your former spouse should act in a certain way supports Darkness Thoughts. Even when expectations are reasonable, such thoughts lead to frustration because you will be setting up expectations the other person may choose not to meet. You will be disappointed and your former spouse will likely be agitated by your expectations rather than being cooperative.

On the other hand, I cannot change my former spouse's behavior no matter how wrong it seems, is an In-the-Light Thought. It acknowledges the reality that you are not responsible for your former spouse's choices. Recognizing that you cannot control your former spouse does not mean you subject yourself or your children to inappropriate or abusive behavior from that person.

I need to assume responsibility for my former spouse's well-being is another Darkness Thought. Divorce relieves you of any responsibility for that person other than court-ordered support. Continuing to assume further responsibility keeps you emotionally tied to your former spouse.

Examples of In-the-Light Thoughts about a Former Spouse:

- Making an emotional break with my former spouse will help me to move on with my life.
- I cannot assume responsibility for my former spouse's behavior. However, that does not mean I subject my children or myself to an abuse.
- My former spouse's choices don't need to make sense to me.
- I will do my best to have a civil relationship with my former spouse.
- Forgiveness is a decision that frees me.
- I can forgive my former spouse without approving of the behavior I am forgiving.

Concentrated Effort

When it comes to your former spouse, it will likely take concentrated effort to replace Darkness Thoughts with In-the-Light Thoughts. If a thought keeps you tied to the past in a way that hinders your ability to move forward toward a positive life in the promises of God, it is a Darkness Thought. Recognize it, pray for strength and wisdom to replace it, and persist until you succeed.

The Darkness/In-the-Light Thought Principle: Example of a Thought about a Former Spouse

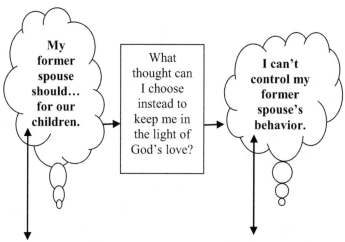

Darkness Outcomes:

- I increase my frustration by continuing to try to control someone I cannot control.
- The children's sense of loss may be intensified by my focus on their other parent's shortcomings.
- My focus on my ex-spouse's behavior brings a spirit of agitation that runs contrary to God's spirit of peace.

In-the-Light Outcomes:

- Accepting that I cannot make my children's other parent act a certain way reduces my stress and allows my energies to be focused elsewhere for the good of my children.
- Accepting that I cannot control my ex-spouse helps me to further break emotional bonds with that person.
- Accepting the reality of my ex-spouse's choices does not change that person's behavior, but it does bring more of God's peace to my life and therefore to the lives of my children.

Making Information and Ideas Work

1. What things about your former spouse still ruin your day or get on your nerves?

2. What thoughts do you have that support the answer you gave to question 1?

3. What new thoughts do you need to concentrate on to replace Darkness Thoughts about your former spouse?

Talk with God--Ponder this reading and share your thoughts with God. Listen so that the Holy Spirit might fill you with wisdom and peace. What concrete actions do you need to take based on what God is saying to you?

A righteous man may have many troubles, but the Lord delivers him from them all ...

Psalm 34:19 NIV

Highlights from Chapter 6
Redirect Your Thoughts

1. Darkness Thoughts are self-defeating thoughts that take away personal power and leave a victim mindset. They are thoughts that are distant from the promises and spirit of God. Repeated, these thoughts carve a rut that prevents moving past the fall-out of divorce.

2. In-the-Light Thoughts inspire healthy growth even in undesirable circumstances. Thoughts that encourage learning from mistakes and that are rooted in hope will help you to move past divorce. Such thoughts lead to the healing, peace, and joy that are consistent with the promises of God.

3. Thinking about thoughts allows for identifying and replacing those that prevent healing and peace.

4. You do not have to accept a thought just because it occurs.

5. Changing to an In-the-Light Thought from a Darkness Thought takes practice. Repeat the new thought as needed until it replaces the Darkness Thought.

6. Since thoughts are related to emotions and to behavior, shifting to In-the-Light Thoughts can have the ripple effects of helping you feel better and of helping you to make better choices.

7. The Darkness Thought that God is angry with you because your marriage ended may cause you to distance yourself from God or try to earn your way back into his favor. Neither action leads to healing. Ignoring God leaves emptiness and trying to be perfect leaves frustration.

8. In-the-Light Thoughts about God help you to grow closer to God thus enabling you to draw from his strength as you work to renew your life after divorce.

9. Thoughts that praise God are In-the-Light Thoughts and have amazing power to bring peace, even when praising seems like an unlikely thing to do.

10. Darkness Thoughts, such as believing divorce represents the end of all happiness, actually block the ability to find happiness.

11. Thinking that single people need a mate to make them whole may result in seeking a mate before working through the fallout of divorce.

12. Proper support and love help children of divorce to adjust.

13. The longer you dwell on regrets, the more they become like quicksand that sucks you downward into the mire of the past.

14. Faith in God offers you a solid place to stand while shifting from thinking in hindsight to casting a vision for your future.

15. Darkness Thinking says you failed. In-the-Light Thinking tells you that the past does not have to predict your future.

16. Redefining thoughts about your former spouse is a part of letting go of the past.

17. By taking control of thoughts, you can keep your former spouse from being able to continue to push your buttons.

18. Self-reflection, talking with God, and reading the Word of God can help you make the transition from Darkness Thoughts to In-the-Light Thoughts.

CHAPTER 7

CHOOSE YOUR ACTIONS

Choosing actions that move you away from the brokenness of divorce and toward a greater sense of well-being requires thinking about what you are doing.

When you decide to seek peace and renewal after the breakdown of your relationship, you are deciding to make healthy decisions about how you act. To do that, you must first become aware of what you are doing. Next, you have to determine if your actions are helping you to heal or holding you back. Deciding how your actions affect your ability to break free of the past and move on with your life gives you a decided edge when it comes to recovering from divorce and finding a life of peace.

Staying True to Yourself and God

*For this very reason, make every effort to add to your
faith goodness, and to goodness, knowledge; and to
knowledge, self-control; and to self-control, perseverance; and to perseverance, godliness; and to godliness,
brotherly kindness; and to brotherly kindness, love.
For if you possess these qualities in increasing measure,
they will keep you from being ineffective and unproduc-
tive in your knowledge of our Lord Jesus Christ.*

2 Peter 1:5-8 NIV

Staying Focused

"I do not understand what I do. For what I want to do I
do not do, but what I hate I do," says Paul in Romans 7:15.
It is easy to relate to what Paul is saying. Even when we are
trying, we sometimes mess up. This human condition is especially true when dealing with divorce. Highly emotional
situations may lead to acting in a way that is counterproductive.

Since dealing with a former spouse can be an emotionally loaded experience, it is especially important to pray for
self-control regarding your words, tone of voice, and actions. Self-control requires effort, premeditation, and determination. It may not change how a former spouse acts, but it
will bolster your sense of self-control, self-worth, and confidence.

A prayerfully developed plan for interacting with a former, or soon to be former spouse, can help with standing firm while still acting in the spirit of Christianity. It can help with feeling good about yourself even when your former spouse is being difficult. With Spirit-filled knowledge, self-control, and perseverance, you can act in a way that will redefine your relationship with your previous mate while being true to yourself as a Christian.

Knowing how God would have us treat one another is important when trying to handle divorce in a Christian way. Christ would have us to treat others, even those who have done us wrong, in a respectful way. That does not mean that the other person is respect-worthy, it means our behavior is respectable. Brotherly kindness and Christian love are not the same as tolerating abuse or approving of inappropriate behavior.

Make Every Effort

2 Peter 1:5-8 tells us to make every effort to add goodness, knowledge, self-control, perseverance, godliness, brotherly kindness, and love to our faith. Clearly, God wants us to choose our actions. Healing power lies in making every effort to choose actions that keep you true to God and to yourself as you work through divorce.

Walking with Christ through divorce is like sailing through rough waters at night guided by a lighthouse. Continue to seek God while working through the darkness. Study his word, seek him in prayer, and grow through the support of a Christian community. God loves and will sustain you as you seek to follow his way in your actions.

Making Information and Ideas Work

1. In what areas do you have the most trouble with your actions toward your former spouse?

2. What does it mean to handle your divorce with behavior that is respect worthy?

Talk with God--Ponder this reading and share your thoughts with God. Listen so that the Holy Spirit might fill you with wisdom and peace. What concrete actions do you need to take based on what God is saying to you?

Self-control requires effort, premeditation, and determination. It may not change how a former spouse acts, but it will bolster your sense of self-control, self-worth, and confidence.

Changing Dynamics with Your Former Spouse

Each one should test his own actions.
Then he can take pride in himself,
without comparing himself to somebody else,
for each one should carry his own load.

Galatians 6:4-5 NIV

Divorcing means, I am me and you are you, and even if we must interact about our children, we now have separate lives. Making this shift requires changes to the dynamics of your relationship. This is important whether your divorce has already occurred or is pending. You have the power and right to define your role in those changes. You cannot control your former spouse, but you can set guidelines that support the concept that because of divorce, you are now two independent people.

Setting Guidelines for Your Actions

Setting guidelines for how you will allow yourself to be treated when dealing with your former spouse isn't an act of hostility. It isn't about being mean and it isn't un-Christian. It is instead a way to protect yourself as you establish yourself as an independent person.

Setting guidelines for yourself regarding your new relationship with your former spouse does two things. First, it clarifies your own thinking regarding how you will act in relationship to your former spouse. Second, it gives you a framework for how you will allow yourself to be treated by your former spouse.

Claim Your Rights

One way to identify personal guidelines for dealing with your former spouse is by identifying and claiming your rights as an independent person. Rights can include many things, from the right to respectful treatment, to the right to make your own decisions. It is challenging but especially important to establish your rights when you have been married to someone who violated your rights.

Claiming your rights frees you from old unhealthy patterns in your marriage relationship. Interestingly, when you learn to claim your own rights, you will find it easier to honor your former spouse's rights. Below are examples of rights a person might choose to claim.

I Have a Right to
- Feel as I feel.
- Keep communications with my ex civil but business-like.
- Cut ties to my ex as much as possible.
- Cease to rely on my ex.
- Cease to allow my ex to rely on me.
- Minimize contact with my former mate.
- Choose my beliefs.
- Want a good life.
- Manage my own money.
- Choose what I value.
- Set limits on how people treat me.

- Take care of myself.
- Make my own decisions.
- Walk with Christ.

Clarify Your Responsibilities

Another way to identify personal guidelines is to consider responsibilities. This means carrying your own load and drawing lines about what is not your responsibility. Randy offers us an example.

Randy felt guilty for ending his marriage. Every time his former wife called and asked him to complete a repair at her house, he would. This continued for some time after their divorce. Randy finally decided it was no longer his responsibility to do her chores since he was no longer married to this woman. The next time she called, he politely told her that he would no longer be available to do her repairs. By declaring his freedom from what was now her responsibility, he drew a line that allowed him to break a tie to the past.

To set responsibility guidelines for yourself, first list what you determine to be your responsibilities. Second, make a list of what is not your responsibility. Items on the lists may range from duties such as being responsible for maintaining your own car, to relationship issues such as not being responsible for your former spouse's happiness. These lists will help you set guidelines for your own actions and help you claim and communicate what is and is not your responsibility.

Allow Consequences

Violations of your personal guidelines need logical consequences. Consequences are outcomes and are not vindictive or hateful. Consequences reinforce your limits. For example, if your former spouse calls and says come bail me out of jail for drinking and driving, you may decide that is not your responsibility. By not assuming responsibility for the outcomes of your former spouse's behavior, you allow your former spouse to experience natural consequences.

The Benefit of Setting Guidelines

Setting new guidelines for your relationship with your former spouse takes effort and practice. It may even increase the tension in the relationship at first. Yet, being intentional about setting and keeping your guidelines has many pay-offs.

Guidelines say, "I will not be pushed around." Claiming your rights, clarifying responsibilities, and then setting guidelines to redefine your relationship with your former spouse, may not be received graciously at first--especially if your new stance keeps your former from being able to manipulate you. He or she may simply not be happy with you. Yet, if you respect yourself by holding on to your personal guidelines, while acting in a respectful way to your former spouse, you increase your chances of making positive strides in redefining your relationship.

Implementing personal guidelines makes communication more honest and direct. It also helps to protect you from 'shoulds.' For example, you should loan me money or you should make my car payments until our divorce is final.

The self-control gained by claiming your rights and clarifying responsibilities helps keep you from getting sucked into game playing and manipulative behavior. You choose your responses rather than reacting based on how your for-

178

mer spouse is treating you. Healthy patterns that claim your independence can replace old unhealthy patterns that developed in marriage.

Breaking Free

Each person has a right to identify personal guidelines for a relationship. Depending on your choices, this may mean that you will no longer be available to change the oil in your former spouse's car. When dealing with a soon-to-be former mate with a substance abuse problem, it may mean drawing lines in your relationship that protect you from the fallout of the substance abuse. It may mean claiming your right to your own opinion without accepting correction from your ex. It may mean refusing to allow further emotional and physical abuse. At the same time, respecting your ex's independence is important if you hope to gain respect for your own.

A God-Given Right

God gives you the right to decide who you are and to teach others what is acceptable behavior toward you. God gives you the right to identify and communicate what you will and will not put up with from your ex. Personal guidelines help clarify rights and responsibilities in your own mind allowing you to become more comfortable with the new relationship and build your confidence as an independent person. Redefining your relationship with your ex is critical if you are to move forward to an independent life.

Making Information and Ideas Work

1. Make a list of things that are your responsibility as a single person.

   Examples:

   I am responsible for my own well-being.

   I am responsible for the consequences of my own decisions.

   I am responsible for my healing from divorce.

2. List several things regarding your former mate that are no longer your responsibility.

   Examples:

   I am not responsible for my former spouse's happiness.

   I am not responsible for picking up her dry cleaning.

   I am not responsible for his diet.

3. Based on your lists of responsibilities, on what personal guidelines do you still need to act?

4. Make a list of at least five of your rights.

5. What does your list of rights suggest about personal guidelines you need to set?

Talk with God--Ponder this reading and share your thoughts with God. Listen so that the Holy Spirit might fill you with wisdom and peace. What concrete actions do you need to take based on what God is saying to you?

Communicating with Your Former Spouse

*The tongue has the power of life and death,
and those who love it will eat its fruit.*

Proverbs 18:21 NIV

The Stomach Churning Jitters

Stomach churning, teeth gritting, and insides trembling, I had the jitters. Talking with the person who was soon to be my former spouse was rattling. I tried not to lose control, but it was not easy.

The hard thing about talking with your former spouse is that the emotions and the dynamics of your history together color your ability to communicate without at least one of you running the risk of feeling hurt, hostile, or frustrated. Your past relationship filters what you say to each other and what you hear from each other. The greater the tension between the two of you, the greater the effort it takes to handle communications with your former spouse effectively.

The Fruit of Words

Words are powerful. Words can stir people up or calm them down. "Reckless words pierce like a sword, but the tongue of the wise brings healing," says Proverbs 12:18. The way you communicate with your former spouse is important during your separation and divorce. Assuming a completely passive role can leave you feeling like a doormat. Being aggressive can set you up for further frustration and can hinder communication.

The challenge is to behave in a way that honors God, is healthy for you, and develops a more neutral and less emotional relationship with your former spouse. This requires taking charge of yourself and making constructive choices about the way you communicate. Setting guidelines for your communications with your former spouse can help you do that.

Setting Communication Guidelines

You cannot control the words and reactions of your former spouse, but you can choose your own words and reactions. Doing so is easier if you plan ahead and set guidelines for your role in communicating with your former spouse. Here are seven strategies that may help if you need to set communication guidelines.

Eliminate Unnecessary Contact

"He called or texted me several times a day," says Ann. "I finally told him I would only respond to messages and calls I received from him after 6 PM. He kept texting me throughout the day for a while until he finally realized I was serious."

If your former spouse is prone to contacting you frequently, it is within your rights to set guidelines regarding how often, when, and for what purposes that contact may occur. You have the right to limit contact to what is essential for the good of children or settling business issues. Set your desired guidelines and stick to them.

Take Charge of You

Stop, reflect, and choose your own words. If your former spouse says things that agitate you and you react with agitation, you are allowing your former spouse to be in charge of you. Choosing your own words rather than reacting allows you to maintain control of yourself.

One technique is to anticipate conversations and to plan your words. Doing so helps you to stay in charge of yourself and to have more control in the conversation. It does not guarantee that the other person will react as you want or expect. Remember, it takes two to fuel the fire of an argument.

"A fool shows his annoyance at once, but a prudent man overlooks an insult," says Proverb 12:16. Overlooking an insult may feel like you are letting the other person win. Nothing could be further from the truth.

Keep Your Focus

Taking charge of communications with your former spouse is easier if you are clear on why you are communicating in the first place. What is the business-at-hand for this interaction? The answer allows you to keep focused on that purpose and not get sidetracked into debates or unrelated arguments.

Own Your Problems and Choose Your Words

John has to talk with his former wife frequently regarding their children. She is volatile and often blows up with him on the phone. Her attacks are becoming more frequent.

John's wife's behavior is creating a problem for John. Despite the fact that she starts the attacks, John owns the problem of not wanting to be the target of her yelling anymore. John has three basic ways he can handle this situation. First, he can continue to be passive and just take what she dishes out. Second, he can launch a counterattack such as, "You are so immature with your crazy yelling." Third, he can in a calm and respectful tone, establish a communication guideline.

John's first option just avoids dealing with his problem. His second option may make the problem worse because any complaint beginning with the word "you" is prone to a defensive response. Furthermore, being verbally aggressive with a counterattack inflames the relationship. James 3:5-6 compares the tongue to a spark that can set a great forest on fire. Blowing off steam with inappropriate words or verbal attacks may feel good for the moment, but it serves neither you nor God.

John would do well to set a guideline to address this communication problem with his former wife. For example, John might say in a firm but calm way, "I will only talk on the phone when I am not being yelled at." This states John's position and expectation in a way that does not attack his former wife. If that approach is not effective, John may need to set a consequence, "I'm being yelled at now. I'll call back later." By using "I" instead of "you" as the subject of his complaint, John will have a better chance of getting his former spouse to listen.

Stating your position rather than making accusations does not guarantee the desired results, but it allows you to stand up for yourself while increasing the chance that the other person will hear what you are saying. The point is to attack the issue not the person.

Monitor Your Body Language

Tone and body language communicate volumes. If your words are non-threatening but your tone is aggressive and your eyes are shooting darts, you are likely to trigger an aggressive response. "A man of knowledge uses words with restraint, and a man of understanding is even-tempered," says Proverbs 17:27. Your voice and expressions are as important to having an even temper, as are the words you say. In the same vein, staring at the floor with your shoulders slumped does not communicate confidence.

Remember Your Nose

"Don't cut off your nose to spite your face," is an old saying. It serves as a reminder that being spiteful to others often has a backlash. Verbally striking out with hostile words has the repercussion of feeding malice in your heart. (See Ephesians 4:29-32.) Hostile feelings will interfere with your ability to communicate effectively with your former spouse as well as with your healing. Worse yet, hostile feelings keep you from feeling the peace of God.

Pray for Strength, Wisdom, and a Calm Spirit

Claim the words of Psalm 16:7-8, which says, "I will bless the Lord who guides me; even at night my heart instructs me. I know the Lord is always with me. I will not be shaken, for he is right beside me."

The Power of the Tongue

Communications are an important part of your actions when it comes to healing from divorce. The words you say and how you say them have significant impact on your ability to get thoughts across to those you deal with during and after divorce. Choose your communications wisely. "...he who holds his tongue is wise," says Proverbs 10:19.

Making Information and Ideas Work

1. How would you describe your communications with your former spouse? Do you feel like a doormat? Hostile and aggressive? Effective? Why?

2. Do you allow your actions toward your former mate to be determined by his or her behavior? If so, how?

3. Have you set personal guidelines for communications with your former spouse? If not, what personal guidelines would you like to set?

4. Think of something you need to say to your former spouse. Next, write that thought into an "I" statement that gives your position without being aggressive toward your former spouse.

5. Stand in front of a mirror and say the statement you wrote in number 4. Do you look calm or aggressive? What body language elements do you need to work on improving when dealing with your former spouse?

6. How can you use the power of the tongue to help you heal?

7. How will claiming Psalm 16:7-8 help you to communicate more effectively with your former spouse?

Talk with God--Ponder this reading and share your thoughts with God. Listen so that the Holy Spirit might fill you with wisdom and peace. What concrete actions do you need to take based on what God is saying to you?

> *I will bless the Lord who guides me;*
> *even at night my heart instructs me.*
> *I know the Lord is always with me.*
> *I will not be shaken,*
> *for he is right beside me.*
>
> Psalm 16:7-8 NIV

Refreshing Yourself

For you created my inmost being; you knit me together in my mother's womb. I praise you because I am fearfully and wonderfully made; your works are wonderful, I know that full well. My frame was not hidden from you when I was made in the secret place. When I was woven together in the depths of the earth, your eyes saw my unformed body. All the days ordained for me were written in your book before one of them came to be.

Psalm 139:13-16 NIV

The One and Only You

It is a marvel that the God of all creation designed each person with a unique combination of traits. No one is just like you. From abilities to interests, talents and skills, God gifted you in a special way valued by him.

It only makes sense to believe that God intends for you to make the most of your talents, interests, and personality. Developing yourself in this way requires assuming responsibility for yourself and your growth. God means for you to seek him and to act to make your life happen. "Ask and it will be given to you; seek and you will find; knock and the door will be opened to you," says Matthew 7:7.

Build Your Confidence

Self-doubt is a natural outgrowth of a marriage that did not work. Working through times of self-doubt by acting to develop yourself will help build your confidence. Building your confidence will not only result in feeling better about yourself, it will also improve your relationships with others. Even on those days when confidence in yourself fails, you can have confidence in belonging to Christ. "Therefore, if anyone is in Christ, he is a new creation; the old has gone, the new has come!" says 2 Corinthians 5:17.

Move Yourself up on the Priority List

Marriage can bring many blessings, but also many demands. Often personal interests and goals give way to family commitments and spouse interests and goals. Children still need an appropriate place in your priorities, but don't lose sight of making your own growth and development a priority too. Nurturing yourself is not only self-renewing, it also enables you to support your children better and to maintain healthier relationships with the other people in your life.

Discover Yourself Again

Take a fresh look at yourself. What were your interests, goals, and aspirations before you married? Which ones fell through the cracks during your marriage? Who are you now? Who do you want to be? Reflecting on the answers to the questions can help to identify the gifts and interests you wish to develop now. Exploring the answers to these questions and setting new goals for personal growth is a positive way to move forward with your life.

Have you always wanted to join a community softball league? Do you want to return to school? Do you want to learn to assert yourself better? How about pursuing a new hobby or serving through your church or community?

As an independent person, you have the freedom to discover who you are and who you want to become. Growing and developing in this way can help you build a strong sense of yourself as a single person. Developing your sense of self is invigorating. Embrace this exciting adventure and discover what an interesting person you truly are.

Making Information and Ideas Work
1. What were you like before you married?

2. What interests or parts of you went by the wayside while you were married?

3. What parts of you do you want to develop now?

4. What hobbies would you like to develop?

5. What things would you like to achieve with your life?

Talk with God--Ponder this reading and share your thoughts with God. Listen so that the Holy Spirit might fill you with wisdom and peace. What concrete actions do you need to take based on what God is saying to you?

Taking Care of Your Health

*Do you not know that your body is a temple of the Holy
Spirit, who is in you, whom you have received from God?
You are not your own; you were bought at a price.
Therefore honor God with your body.*

1 Corinthians 6:19-20 NIV

Since God put so much into designing you, it should be
clear that taking care of yourself is not selfish. Taking care
of yourself is being responsible to God. Only by taking care
of yourself will you be able to live with the fullness and
purpose God has planned for you.

Health and Divorce

The emotions and trauma of divorce can have significant
impact on your health. Sleeping and eating patterns may become disturbed. Tight budgets may restrict health care.
Feeling blue or simply being busy may reduce motivation or
time available to exercise. Stress takes its physical and men-
tal toll.

Researchers from Johns Hopkins University and the University of Chicago found a correlation between divorce and
health problems, noting that the detrimental effects on
health can still be evident after many years.[4] Results of this
study are like a red flag saying take action regarding your
health. Chances are that by working through the emotional

issues of divorce, and by taking care of your physical health, you stand to minimize the negative impact of divorce on your body.

Emotions and Health

Our emotions, thoughts, behaviors, and physical body intertwine. If bottled up, the emotions of divorce must surely take their toll. In his book, ***What You Don't Know May Be Killing You***, Dr. Don Colbert says, "prolonged attitudes of fear and anxiety…can actually lead to adrenal exhaustion, fatigue, anxiety and panic attacks, irritable bowel syndrome, and tension headaches, in addition to other symptoms."[5]

It is crucial that you work through emotions and tend to your health in general during and after divorce. Adequate exercise is a stress reliever as well as a boost for your physical and emotional health. Brisk walking is an excellent option for most people. Check with your doctor.

Divorce may have a positive impact on health if a person is escaping an abusive relationship or highly stressful situation. In these cases, divorce may increase physical safety as well as relieve stress. Even so, being mindful of your health is good for you and can increase your sense of well-being throughout life.

Nutrition

Diets may give way to packaged foods and fast foods when going through divorce or living as a single person. If fresh vegetables and fruits have all but disappeared from your diet, take heed and find ways to eat healthier meals. Talk with a nutritionist or your doctor or tap the Internet for help.

Food for the Soul

Nourishing your soul is just as important as nourishing your body. Knowing you are valued and valuable is important to your emotional and physical health. When Jesus rose from the tomb and appeared to Mary Magdalene, he called her by name (John 20:16). The interaction was personal. Knowing that Jesus also knows you by name is awe-inspiring. That knowledge speaks to the personal relationship he wants with you. The mindset and feelings that flow from embracing this concept are supportive and healing.

Getting it All Together

Dealing with the stresses and issues of divorce can take its toll on your health, but you can take steps to manage the degree of impact. By working through the emotional aspects of divorce, growing in God, and taking charge of your physical health, you stand to improve your overall wellness. Being healthy adds to your strength and sense of well-being as you work through the issues of divorce.

Making Information and Ideas Work

1. Has divorce affected your sleeping habits?

2. Has divorce affected your eating habits?

3. Are you getting proper exercise?

4. Are you nourishing yourself on the Word of God?

5. Review your answers to the previous questions and then write personal goals for protecting your health.

Talk with God--Ponder this reading and share your thoughts with God. Listen so that the Holy Spirit might fill you with wisdom and peace. What concrete actions do you need to take based on what God is saying to you?

Helping Children Cope with Divorce

God-loyal people, living honest lives,
make it much easier for their children.

Proverbs 20:7 THE MESSAGE

"It is hard enough that she left me but how could she do this to our children," said Carl. "She has turned our lives upside down by divorcing me."

Carl faces what many parents face – the challenge of helping his children adjust in a healthy way to the divorce of their parents while at the same time dealing with his own emotions and adjustments. Ideally, both parents will set aside their own agendas and work together for the good of the children. Of course, that is not always the case. Even if you are a single parent flying solo in your human efforts, you can still have a positive impact in helping your children to adapt and thrive. God the father, the greatest parent ever, will always be present for you and your children.

If you seek God's wisdom and guidance, and do everything you can to support the adjustment of your children, God will see you through what you cannot do on your own. Divorce creates trying times, even for adult children, but it does not have to scar your children. By strengthening their sense of security; keeping communication open; setting guidelines for your own behavior; and by nurturing your children's faith in God, you can have a positive life-long impact. While each family situation has its own dimensions, here are some things to consider when helping your children adjust to separation and the ongoing impact of divorce.

Keep Kids Feeling Safe and Snug

By God's design, it is the parents' responsibility to provide for their children and to keep them safe. Understandably, children have an especially strong need for this security and love when adapting to situations impacted by their parents' divorce. Children are always on the receiving end of a divorce--it is rarely what they would choose, and yet they can do nothing about it.

Things like where they will live and whether it is still okay to love both parents can concern children. Over time, other issues arise including how to handle holidays and special occasions like birthdays and graduations. By simply reminding yourself that helping your children to feel secure is important, you can focus more on making it happen. Below are some things to keep in mind.

Make Home Feel Safe

Remember, if you appear out of control to children, their world does not feel safe. As the adult in the household, you set the atmosphere in the home. If you're flipping out in the presence of your children, or screaming at your former spouse over the phone, the kids are unlikely to feel safe. Furthermore, having a short fuse with your kids does not help them to adjust to divorce. Find constructive ways to release your stress.

Free Children to Love Both Parents

Don't put children in the position of having to choose one parent over the other, even indirectly.

Assure Children That Both Parents Love Them

By definition, divorce means two adults no longer live together. From a child's view, this may mean one of my parents left me. It may also mean less time spent with one of the parents.

Despite the changes in living arrangements, it is ideal for each parent to communicate love to the children through both word and action. This said, it is also important to accept that you cannot force the other parent to be as supportive as you might hope. Consult with the appropriate authorities if your children need protection from an abusive parent.

Lift the Question of Responsibility from Children

Since children are me-centered, they may feel like the divorce is their fault. It is not. They need reassurance that no matter what they may have done or not done, the breakdown of a marriage is an adult problem.

Explain Divorce's Impact on Their Lives

The unknown is scarier than any monster that lives under a child's bed. Explain to your children, in an age appropriate way, what divorce will mean to their lives. Where will they live? Will they still see both parents? Will they change schools? And so forth.

Ease Transitions

When the time comes, help children to adjust to the idea that you are going to start to date. Some kids will not like the idea. Others may have the unrealistic expectation that if you find someone else to marry, all of the family's problems will go away. Reassure children that their importance to you will not decrease when you reenter the dating world or marry again.

Keep Communication Open

Listen to your children and honestly address their concerns. Doing so builds your relationship and lets them know they are valued. It also gives you the chance to clear up misconceptions and to help your children deal with divorce in a positive way.

Explain How the New Family Structure Will Work

Ideally, both parents will agree to a plan that focuses on the best interest of the children. Even if your former spouse is not willing to do this, keep your focus on the children's best interest no matter how your former spouse acts. Children need to know such things as how much time they will be spending with each parent, how family traditions will now be handled, and what to expect at holidays.

Encourage Expression of Feelings

Realize children will have a bundle of feelings and may have little in the way of skills to cope with them. Let your children know it is okay to be sad and to talk about their feelings regarding the divorce and the changes it has brought to their lives. Help them to find other safe people they can talk with who will be supportive and not pass judgment on them or the situation. Spend time playing games or doing other activities with them to help develop your relationship and rapport.

Watch for Non-Verbal Communication

Since kids may not always have the insight or words to express their frustrations, there may be nonverbal clues that indicate they are struggling with situations related to divorce--clues such as acting out, withdrawal, or regular stomach aches. Keep in mind that kids need a chance to grieve just as you do. Be patient and connect with your children at these times. Seek professional help if needed.

Expect and Accept Questions

Be prepared to address tough questions and accusations from your children. Anticipate questions so that you are prepared with an age-appropriate and honest response. Don't be defensive. Don't get into mudslinging. You can help your children by letting them get these questions out and by not getting angry as you respond.

Listen with Both Ears

Let one ear listen for what your kids say about the divorce and its spin-offs. Let the other ear listen for the feelings behind the words they say. Listen without interrupting.

The Dilemma of Adult Children of Divorce

Adult children are not immune to the impact of their parents' divorce. In fact, as adults, they may tend to jump into the fray to try to fix their parent's problems, or choose one parent's side over the other. Neither role is likely to have positive outcomes for anybody. Choosing sides has long-term implications for children and can be especially sticky if the parents reconcile. Like youngsters, adult children can feel emotionally uprooted when their family falls apart. Many of the guidelines listed in this section apply to adult children of divorce just as they apply to children who are still dependents.

Divorcing parents may tend to overlook the needs of adult children of divorce thinking that as grown-ups, their children should be able to handle adult issues. Even so, details of the other parent's misdoings can shatter parent images that are at the core of an adult child. Furthermore, using your children as a sounding board recasts their traditional role in the family to a role that may be uncomfortable, even to adult children.

The truth is adult issues take on a new meaning when those adults are your parents. Sharing intimate details of your marriage and sex life with your adult children, just because they are adults, ignores the fact that they are still your children. "For heaven's sake," said Katie, "these are my parents! I just did not need to have that picture in my head."

Set Guidelines for the Good of Your Children

By setting guidelines for the well-being of your children, you establish an outline for your own actions. That outline helps you to manage the spin-off of divorce as it affects your children. Below are some guidelines you can set to help your children adjust to divorce.

Honor the Children's Other Parent

"... parents are the pride of their children" (Proverbs 17:6). Whatever your opinion of your former spouse that person remains the parent of your joint children. Expressing hostility or criticism toward or about that person in front of your children only adds stress to their lives. Kids are smart. If your former spouse is a louse, they will likely figure it out.

Never Use Children as a Bargaining Chip

Using your children as a bargaining chip to manipulate your former spouse is selfish and heartless. Worse yet, it puts the well-being of the child second to your ulterior motives.

Check Your Motives

Don't let the power of your own emotions cloud your judgment regarding your children. For example, withholding visitation with the other parent because you are in conflict with the other parent over adult issues punishes the child unfairly. A positive relationship with both parents reinforces a child's sense of security and well-being.

Never Place Your Children in the Middle of a Conflict

Deal parent to parent. It is unfair to use your child as a messenger when it comes to settling issues between parents, even when the issues relate to the child. If you need to negotiate who will pay for summer camp, do it parent to parent. If you don't want your children visiting their other parent for some reason, deal with it parent to parent. If child support is past due, deal with it through appropriate channels. Do not put children in the middle of adult problems. Colossians 3:21 reminds us, "Fathers, do not embitter your children, or they will become discouraged."

Avoid Using Your Child as Your Confidant

Confiding in your child about your struggles, conflicts, and emotions unduly burdens your child and can add further tension and confusion to his or her life. This is true even with adult children. Find a neutral friend, or counselor who is not emotionally involved with you and your former spouse to use as your confidant.

Don't Speak for Your Child's Other Parent

Know which questions from your kids you can answer and which you need to defer to the other parent. Don't attempt to answer questions for which you have no answers. Why did Daddy leave us is best answered by Daddy. Kindly tell them that they will have to ask Daddy, assuming Daddy is available. Do be sure they know that you love them and will always be there for them.

Stay in Charge of You

Don't allow yourself to be manipulated by your children. Children who are anxious to see you reunite may try to get you and your former spouse back together in any number of ways, including trying to make you feel guilty. Let them know you appreciate their concern but that such decisions belong to the adults. Help them to know that they can adapt and thrive even though they may not be happy with all of the circumstances that come from divorce.

Respect Each Child's Space

Sometimes children just need space. If they are not ready to talk with you at a given time, leave the door open for future conversation. Realize that children are individuals and will therefore handle the divorce in their own way. Do not compare your children.

Teach Your Children

When Moses finished sharing The Ten Commandments with the Israelites, he then told them to do three things. First, "Love the LORD your God with all your heart and with all your soul and with all your strength." Second, keep God's commandments "upon your hearts." Third, "Impress them on your children" (Deuteronomy 6:5-7).

Model Your Faith

One of the best ways to teach your children is to show them the way by your own behavior. If you share with them that your faith sees you through your trials, they will learn the power of faith. If you seek God's wisdom and guidance and teach your children to do the same, you give them an awesome gift. Nothing is more empowering than knowing that the God of all creation will send his Holy Spirit to live in you, strengthen you, and help you grow in his way.

Ephesians 6:4 tells parents not to, "exasperate your children; instead, bring them up in the training and instruction of the Lord." If you believe that God has good things in store for your future, if you trust in him, your example will be a powerful teacher. Your beliefs and your behavior will serve as a positive illustration of faith in action.

Provide a Spiritual Home Base

Fertilize the seeds of faith you plant in your children by giving them a church home. Church ministries for children can reinforce your efforts to reassure them that God is real and loves them very much. The adults children encounter at church also broaden their support network.

Making Information and Ideas Work

1. What are you currently doing to keep your children feeling secure?

2. Look back over the section *Set Guidelines for the Good of Your Children* and circle areas where you need to make improvements. Write your plan for those improvements.

3. What can you do to improve communication with your children?

4. Review and if you elect, sign the *Guidelines for the Good of My Children* contract found at the end of this section.

5. How can you better impress upon your children the life-giving power of a relationship with Christ?

Talk with God--Ponder this reading and share your thoughts with God. Listen so that the Holy Spirit might fill you with wisdom and peace. What concrete actions do you need to take based on what God is saying to you?

Love the LORD your God with all your heart and with all your soul and with all your strength.

These commandments that I give you today are to be upon your hearts.

Impress them on your children.

Talk about them when you sit at home and when you walk along the road, when you lie down and when you get up.

Deuteronomy 6:5-7 NIV

Guidelines for the Good of My Children

My Contract with Myself

Don't let the power of your emotions cloud your judgment in a way that has a negative impact on your children. Decide to set standards for your behavior regarding your child's other parent. Set these standards for yourself no matter how your former spouse may act. You may wish to copy this commitment contract for your children's other parent. Tell him or her that you are making these decisions for the good of your children. It will be up to the other parent to decide whether to do the same.

I commit to keeping the following guidelines for the good of my children:

1. I will not speak ill of my children's other parent when within hearing distance of my children.
2. I will never use my children as a bargaining chip to manipulate their other parent.
3. I will never place my children in the middle of my conflicts with their other parent. I will deal adult to adult.
4. I will not use any of my children as my confidant.
5. I will not punish my children by withholding visitation with their other parent.
6. I will not try to speak on behalf of their other parent.
7. I will not allow my children to manipulate me with guilt.

_____   _____

Signature   Date

Highlights from Chapter 7
Choose Your Actions

1. Deciding how your actions influence your ability to break free of the past and move on with your life gives you an edge when it comes to recovering from divorce.

2. You cannot control the words of your former spouse. You can choose your own words rather than reacting.

3. Treating someone with respect when that person has done you wrong does not mean that the other person is respect worthy--it means your behavior is respectable.

4. Brotherly kindness and Christian love is not the same as allowing abuse or tolerating inappropriate behavior.

5. It helps to think through situations before they occur and to make decisions about how you want to act before you are in the heat of a conflict.

6. Setting personal guidelines for yourself is extremely helpful in redefining your relationship with your former spouse.

7. It is okay if your former spouse does not initially receive your personal guidelines graciously, especially when accustomed to being able to manipulate you.

8. Respecting your former spouse's personal guidelines is important if you hope to gain respect for your own.

9. Being verbally aggressive with your former spouse inflames the relationship.

10. Standing strong in asserting yourself is important during your separation and divorce.

11. When interacting with your former spouse, keep your focus on the purpose of the interaction and do not get sidetracked into debates or unrelated arguments.

12. Stating your position rather than making accusations allows you to stand up for yourself while increasing the chance that the other person will hear what you say.

13. The words we say and how we say them have significant impact on our ability to get our thoughts across.

14. The God of all creation designed you with a purpose he specifically ordained. Being who he intended you to be as an individual, requires taking a fresh look at yourself.

15. As an independent person, you have the freedom to discover who you are and who you want to become.

16. Working through times of self-doubt by developing yourself will build your confidence.

17. Taking charge of your physical health adds to your strength and sense of well-being as you work through the issues of divorce.

18. Divorce creates trying times, even for adult children, but it does not have to scar your children.

19. By strengthening your children's sense of security; keeping communication open; setting and keeping guidelines for their benefit; and by nurturing your child's faith in God, you can have a positive life-long impact.

20. Set and keep guidelines for the good of your children. Doing so can help keep your children from being negatively affected by your relationship with their other parent.

CHAPTER 8

CONSIDER WHAT'S NEXT

As you work to close earlier chapters of your life, it is also time to consider the world of opportunity that awaits you.

Congratulations! You've come a long way since you started this book. You are finding the power within yourself and in your relationship with God to help you move forward with your life in a positive way.

Let your success in coming this far motivate you to continue. It is time to assess your progress and to reflect on where you are now. As you work to close earlier chapters of your life, it is also time to consider the world of opportunity that awaits you.

Where Are You Now?

*How much better to get wisdom than gold,
to choose understanding rather than silver!*

Proverbs 16:16 NIV

The self-assessment below consists of some questions to help you think about how far you have come and where you want to go. It is not a scientifically researched test so there are no wrong answers.

Progress Self-Assessment

Read the questions below and evaluate your current progress on a scale of 1-5 with 5 being YES and 1 being NO. Write your number to the right of each question. Assessing yourself at a 2, 3, or 4 means you are making progress toward your goal. Any progress is good. Be honest and mark answers according to your first impulse.

Taking Charge of My Life
Have I accepted divorce as my reality? 4
Do I feel a sense of control in my life? 3
Am I committed to healing remaining divorce wounds? 5
Am I adapting to divorce-related changes in my life? 4
Am I making sound choices about life change? 5

Renewing My Spirit and Soul

Do I accept that God loves me as I am? 5
Have I accepted God's forgiveness if needed? 5
Am I reliant on God instead of angry with God? 5
Do I talk with God honestly and regularly? 3
Do I know God has a plan for me? 3

Untying the Emotional Knot

Do I recognize my emotions as normal? 3
Do I understand the emotional vs. legal divorce? 4
Am I dealing effectively with roadblocks? 3
Do I accept emotional flare-ups as normal? 3
Have I made a defining break with my ex? 4
Have I let go of trying to understand my former spouse? 5
Do I have a realistic perspective on my marriage? 5

Looking Inside

Have I worked through feelings about my former spouse? 4
Have I worked through loss and grief? 3
Am I overcoming feelings of rejection? 4
Am I conquering fear? 3
Is my sense of loneliness diminishing? 1
Am I committed to focus on healing before dating? 4
Am I making a point to choose joy and laughter? 3

Casting Away Stones

Have I stopped blaming my former spouse? 4
Have I moved past feeling like a victim? 4
Am I over the urge for revenge? 5
Have I appropriately released anger related to divorce? 3
Have I let go of the pains of un-forgiveness? 4

Redirecting My Thoughts
Am I choosing In-the-Light thoughts about
  God?
  Marriage and Divorce?
  Singleness?
  Circumstances?
  My Former Spouse?

Am I Choosing Actions that Support the Following:
Successfully coping with daily life? 4
Staying true to myself? 4
Setting personal guidelines for dealing with my ex? 4
Nourishing and refreshing myself? 3
Taking care of my health? 3
Helping my children cope with divorce? 4

What Did You Learn?

The fact that you were willing to complete this self-assessment is a positive sign that you are conscientious about finding peace after divorce. Your next step is to review your self-ratings and determine what you need to work on next. If you rated yourself a 1 on an item, it is an area in which you see yourself needing more work. If you rated yourself a 2, 3, or 4 on an item, then you are growing and you can continue to set goals for moving forward in that area. A rating of 5 suggests you are currently feeling very good about your progress in a given area.

Healing from divorce is much like constructing a building. A partially built building, although not yet complete, is a sign of progress. As with any construction project, it is important to know where you are in the building process so you can decide what to do next.

Making Information and Ideas Work

1. Reflecting on your self-assessment, in what general areas have you progressed the most?

2. What area of achievement has meant the most to you?

   Learning to live on my own again

3. In what areas do you most need to continue working?

   loneliness — how do you make it go away!

Talk with God--Ponder this reading and share your thoughts with God. Listen so that the Holy Spirit might fill you with wisdom and peace. What concrete actions do you need to take based on what God is saying to you?

Finding Purpose in Your Life

*It's in Christ that we find out who we are and what we are
living for. Long before we first heard of Christ and got
our hopes up, he had his eye on us, had designs on us for
glorious living, part of the overall purpose
he is working out in everything and everyone.*

Ephesians 1:11-12 THE MESSAGE

God Has a Purpose for Your Life

Divorce can leave you wondering who you are and why
you are living. Rest assured your life has a purpose. In fact
Ephesians 1:11-12 states that you have a very important
purpose. God did not create you just so you could exist.
Purpose in God is about living a life of spiritual vitality.
Don't settle for anything less.

Is it Safe to Accept God's Purpose for My Life?

Not only is it safe, it is a relief. It answers the question of
why you are on earth. You don't have to be afraid because
God loves you. We believe that whatever purpose God calls
you to will fill you with spiritual blessing.

So What is My Purpose?

God's GPS directs you to God's purpose for your life. This
is not a global positioning system, but is a very special GPS-
-God's Positioning System. The Bible tells us how to posi-

216

tion ourselves to be in God's purpose. Just follow the GPS below.

> G = Grow to be Best Friends with God
> P = Partner with People
> S = Super-Size your Spiritual Life

Grow to be Best Friends with God

First stop on the journey to finding your purpose is to become friends with God and to know he is with you wherever the road leads. In fact, this is in itself a part of God's purpose for you. God loves you and wants you to love him right back with your whole heart, soul and mind (Matthew 22:37-38).

Say Yes to God's Gift. God wants to be the deepest friend of your heart. He paid a tremendous price to let you know that. "For God so loved the world that he gave his one and only Son, that whoever believes in him shall not perish but have eternal life" (John 3:16). Because God loves you, he offers you his grace. Grace means there is nothing you can do to deserve God's love, but he gives it to you anyway. When you say yes to Christ, God wipes your slate clean giving you a fresh new beginning.

Live in the Spirit. God gives you his Holy Spirit to live inside of you and guide you in his way. "But he who unites himself with the Lord is one with him in spirit" (1 Corinthians 6:17). Life's travails won't disappear, but life will change for the better because God is with you to guide you through life's challenges. Growing in the Holy Spirit brings "love, joy, peace, patience, kindness, goodness, faithfulness, gentleness and self-control" (Galatians 5:22-23).

217

Partner with People

Love Others. Part of God's purpose is for you to love others (Matthew 22:39). Loving others for God is not about how you feel as a human. It is better than that. It is instead a decision to act in a way that shows God's love to others. That's love with a purpose. It is amazing how achieving this purpose in your life lifts your spirit and shifts your focus from yourself and your own problems. Showing God's love to others intensifies an awareness of the love of God in your own life.

Hang out with Christians. Spending time with other Christians is another way to partner with God's people. It has two big pay-offs. First, spending time with other believers is nourishing. It strengthens you as a believer and gives you a chance to receive support and to support others. "Two are better than one, because they have a good return for their work: If one falls down, his friend can help him up" (Ecclesiastes 4:9-10). Second, fellowship with other Christians enhances your ability to function as a part of the body of Christ. Combining your gifts with the gifts of other Christians helps you better to serve your purpose. "Now you are the body of Christ, and each one of you is a part of it" (1 Corinthians 12:27).

Super-Size Your Spiritual Life

Seek to Know God Better. God's power and grace are transforming and empowering. God invites us to join him in his purposes. That's amazing because what God can accomplish is phenomenal. Remember, God "is able to do immeasurably more than all we ask or imagine, according to his power that is at work within us," (Ephesians 3:20). The

218

things we dream of pale by comparison to God's purposes for us. "Put on your new nature, and be renewed as you learn to know your Creator and become like him" (Colossians 3:10 NLT).

<u>*Rejoice.* Since God offers you life after death, it makes sense that he also offers you life after divorce.</u> Seeking your purpose gives meaning to your existence and helps redirect your life away from the past and toward glorious living in Christ. As Ephesians says, "It's in Christ that we find out who we are and what we are living for" (Ephesians 1:11 The Message).

> ... *Forgetting what is behind and straining toward what is ahead, I press on toward the goal to win the prize for which God has called me heavenward in Christ Jesus.*
>
> Philippians 3:13-14 NIV

Making Information and Ideas Work

1. What does it mean to your life purpose to have God as your best friend?

2. How can serving others promote God's purpose for you while lifting your own burdens?

3. What benefits can you gain by connecting with other Christians?

4. How does renewing your life in Christ relate to renewing your life after divorce?

5. Re-read the scripture from Ephesians 1:11-12. (See page 216.) What does it mean to you?

Talk with God--Ponder this reading and share your thoughts with God. Listen so that the Holy Spirit might fill you with wisdom and peace. What concrete actions do you need to take based on what God is saying to you?

> *Since God offers you life after death, it stands to reason that he also offers you life after divorce.*

Finding Your Future

*And we know that in all things God works for the good of
those who love him, who have been called
according to his purpose.*

Romans 8:28 NIV

Dare to Dream

The future is full of promise. Walk closely with God
and we believe he will give you eyes to see a positive future. He will give you the courage to dream.

Having a dream is the first step toward living that
dream. A dream says--here is a place I would like to be.
Below are some areas where you may want to dream:

- Dream of freedom from the emotional spin-off of
  divorce.
- Dream of fulfilling God's purpose for your life.
- Dream of improving your relationship skills.
- Dream of things you want to do.
- Dream of things you want to achieve.

Turn Dreams into Goals

Dreams require action to become reality. The chances of
turning a dream into a goal and achieving it are best when
the goal is in line with certain factors. In deciding which

dreams you'd like to turn into goals, consider these factors about each dream's potential as a goal:

- **Is it Sound?** Can you achieve this dream given your talents, abilities, and resources?
- **Is it Definable?** Can you begin to visualize a process for achieving it? Is it measurable? Is it a short-term or long-term goal? What steps would you take to achieve it?
- **Is it Healthy?** Would achieving this dream enhance your life and do no harm to yourself or others?
- **Is it Within Your Control?** If you need the cooperation of others, can you get their support? What are the barriers and can you overcome them?
- **Are You Fired-up about It?** Are you motivated to work to achieve this dream?
- **Is it Manageable?** If achieving the dream becomes overwhelming, frustration may override the desire to achieve that goal. It is good to dream big, but big dreams need to be broken into manageable, written objectives or they become overwhelming.

Set Priorities and Make Plans

Prayerfully developing goals empowers you to set your course for the future while under the shelter of God's wings. As Christians, we are to be proactive. "So I say to you: Ask and it will be given to you; seek and you will find; knock and the door will be opened to you" (Luke 11:9). Taking action to set goals and achieve them feels good. Shifting focus from your divorce to your own goals is positive and can help move you to a more joyful and peaceful place.

Making Information and Ideas Work

1. Reflect on your dreams as well as your self-assessment from the last section and choose a dream that you would like to turn into a goal.

2. Evaluate the dream you wrote about in number 1 by thinking about it in terms of the factors listed in the section entitled, *Turn Dreams into Goals*.

3. Make a list of potential barriers to achieving this dream.

4. Is it possible to overcome these barriers? If so, what must you do to overcome them?

5. If your dream seems like it can become a viable goal, then write a sentence that turns the dream into a goal statement. Be specific about what you plan to achieve.

6. Make a list of the steps you will need to take to reach the goal you wrote in number 5. How long will it take you to reach this goal?

7. Work through this process with other dreams as they surface.

Talk with God--Ponder this reading and share your thoughts with God. Listen so that the Holy Spirit might fill you with wisdom and peace. What concrete actions do you need to take based on what God is saying to you?

Before a New Romance

What good is it for a man to gain the whole world,
and yet lose or forfeit his very self?

Luke 9:25 NIV

Doing the work of healing from divorce before becoming romantically involved with another person is like learning to swim before jumping into the deep of the ocean. You might flounder and drown if unprepared, but if equipped with the skills and emotional preparedness to survive, you'll dramatically increase your chances of success.

It can be tempting to stop short of working through total renewal from divorce. Don't yield to that temptation. Persistence will pay off. Walking around wounded does not make you happy, nor does it make you a good catch.

Like a coat of armor, singleness may be used as a shield from the vulnerabilities of another romance. Isolation prevents hurt. As effective as it is to use singleness as a safe haven, fending off the risks of romance also means sacrificing the joys of a romantic relationship.

Choosing Singleness or Marriage

Finding balance and perspective in your life as a single person helps you to be able to decide whether you wish to remain single or seek a marriage partner. This requires self-knowledge; learning more about healthy relationships; and understanding what it means to be at peace with being single. Heal from divorce and then make a prayerful choice about staying single or seeking a marriage partner. Whether or not you find a marriage partner, you will be able to be happy being you.

Ghosts from the Past

Not to be confused with supernatural beings, the word ghost here refers to learned expectations, irritants, and anxieties from past relationships that color reactions and perspectives in current relationships. When we were dating, we decided to call these carry-overs ghosts because it includes things from personal past history or marriages that are haunting and that may negatively affect new relationships. Some ghosts from the past linger in the shadows of a specific memory. Others loom large and are ever-present.

Unresolved ghosts from the past create internal tensions as well as relationship problems. Being able to identify and label them is the first step in being able to minimize their impact. Recognizing ghosts allows for reflecting on the issues they represent and working through those issues until they lose their power. With time and effort, you can become an effective ghost-buster.

Ghosts may be rooted in a past marriage, your birth family, or other relationships. Recognizing your ghosts can help prevent an unhealthy past relationship pattern from transferring into a new relationship. Working to heal old ghosts also makes you feel better.

For example, if you grow up with peers who consistently take advantage of you, it may result in a relationship ghost. You may continue to allow others to take advantage of you, or you may become quick to assume others are taking advantage of you. Knowing how much God values you, and learning respectfully to stand up for your rights, can help to get rid of this ghost. This in turn will help you to be a happier single person and to have better relationships. The more entrenched your ghosts, the more effort it will take to overcome them.

Most people have ghosts to one degree or another. The unresolved collision of two people's ghosts can contribute to relationship problems. Knowing you and your former spouse each have ghosts may help you understand factors that contributed to the dissolution of your marriage.

Relationships can benefit if both people tune into and work on their ghosts together. Understanding each other's ghosts and their origins can help a couple to be more effective in reducing conflicts that result from ghosts of the past. If you find you are unable to work through ghosts of the past on your own, seek professional assistance.

Making Information and Ideas Work

1. Do you have ghosts from your previous marriage? What are they?

2. How do those ghosts affect you?

3. What can you do to take the power away from each of these ghosts?

4. What do the words of Luke 9:25 mean to you as you prepare for dating?

Talk with God--Ponder this reading and share your thoughts with God. Listen so that the Holy Spirit might fill you with wisdom and peace. What concrete actions do you need to take based on what God is saying to you?

Trusting Again

Then Christ will make his home in your hearts as you trust in him. Your roots will grow down into God's love and keep you strong. And may you have the power to understand, as all God's people should, how wide, how long, how high, and how deep his love is.

Ephesians 3:17-18 NLT

Trust is about being able to rely on someone to be honest, fair, and to have integrity. If you trust someone, you believe that person will look out for your best interests. If the person proves trustworthy, then you learn to trust further and the relationship grows. Trustworthiness is expected from the person you marry.

Hurt is a Powerful Teacher

Distrust develops when someone violates a trust, as is often the case in relationships that lead to divorce. The adage, "once burnt shame on you, twice burnt, shame on me," reflects the human need to learn to protect ourselves from people who hurt us. It is natural and wise to become cautious of someone who has violated a trust.

It is wise to know whom to trust and whom not to trust. In Psalms 5:9 David says of his enemies, "Not a word from their mouth can be trusted; their heart is filled with destruction. Their throat is an open grave; with their tongue they speak deceit." When you fail to protect yourself from nontrustworthy people, you open yourself to abuse.

The mistrust learned when the most important person in your life proves not to be trustworthy can result in a hesitancy to trust others and reluctance to develop new relationships. You may also find yourself doubting your own judgment about who can be trusted. Lack of trust can lead to undue reluctance, suspicion, or jealousy in future relationships.

Learning to Trust Again

With eyes wide-open to the risks of being hurt, increasing your ability to trust takes time. Just as not trusting is a learned behavior, it is also possible to learn to trust again.

It's true that the risks of trust are great, but so are the pay-offs. Trust is requisite to having a loving relationship. If difficulty trusting is one of your divorce ghosts, you can make choices that help break through the trust barrier. Below are seven tips that may help with building trust in a relationship.

1. *Recognize and Admit That Trust is One of Your Divorce Ghosts.* Do you find yourself bailing out of relationships when people get too close? Do you tend to be overly suspicious or jealous? Do you have trouble trusting because others have burned you in the past? Recognizing and admitting a problem is the first step toward dealing with it.

2. *Decide to Take Calculated Risks with Trust.* Analyzing situations rather than relying on emotions can help you find a neutral point between trusting too freely because of emotional neediness, and a reluctance to trust because of fear. Learn to trust again by developing trust in friendships where a possible let-down won't have the severe emotional consequence associated with a romance. Doing this is like wading before you enter the deep water. Each time you venture into the water a little further, you build your comfort level. If you get in too deep, stop and access what's happening and see how you can apply what you have learned to help you make wise decisions about whom to trust.

3. *Identify and Confront Your Trust Ghosts.* Ask yourself what specific events happened in the past that make it hard for you to trust now. Even when someone in another relationship is trustworthy, these shadows of previous experiences can cause you to be suspicious and perhaps accusing. Identify your trust ghosts so that you can recognize them for what they are, hurts from the past, not reflections of the people in your current relationships.

4. *Clarify Your Personal Trust Guidelines.* It is important to be clear about what you will and will not accept in your relationships with others. What behavior do you expect when you decide to trust someone? How do you expect to be treated? What do you think are reasonable trust expectations for another person to place on you?

5. *Communicate.* Communication is crucial in any relationship. Remember, you are responsible for your happiness; no one else can assume that responsibility. Know your personal guidelines for friendships and for dating. Communicating them will help you trust yourself more and let others know what constitutes a violation of your trust.

6. *Make a Decision to Live and Learn.* If every violation of your trust sinks you to a new low, you will forever be struggling with trust because untrustworthy people exist. Trustworthy people also exist. A quality relationship with a trustworthy person is valuable and can make it worthwhile to take calculated risks to trust. Make a decision to learn from both your good and bad experiences.

Doing so will groom you to make better decisions in trusting.

7. *Pray for Discernment.* Solomon asked God for a discerning heart to help him govern the people when he assumed the duties of king. God was pleased at his request and promised him a wise and discerning heart (1 Kings 3:9-10). Discernment is the wisdom to make sound judgments. Paul prayed for the Philippians, "so that you may be able to discern what is best..." (Philippians 1:10). You too can pray for discernment. Ask God to help you make sound judgments as you grow in learning to trust more. Discernment will help you assess a relationship more objectively than when the relationship is viewed through the filters of fear or neediness.

Making Information and Ideas Work

1. List your trust ghosts below stating specific things that happened that make it harder for you to trust.

2. Name one small step you can take to stretch yourself a little in the area of trusting someone else.

3. How can communication help you build trust?

Talk with God--Ponder this reading and share your thoughts with God. Listen so that the Holy Spirit might fill you with wisdom and peace. What concrete actions do you need to take based on what God is saying to you?

Creating Level Paths for Dating

Let your eyes look straight ahead,
fix your gaze directly before you.
Make level paths for your feet and
take only ways that are firm.

Proverbs 4:25-26 NIV

Returning to dating after having been married can be both intriguing and intimidating. The desire to find romance may collide with the fear of being hurt. Making level paths for your feet through the dating scene may seem impossible, but it is not. Knowing who you are and having a clear understanding of your expectations regarding dating won't eliminate all risks, but can help keep your feet on firmer ground.

Know Your Goal in Dating

People date for a variety of reasons. Some are healthy; some are not. All incur some risk. If you are clear on why you are dating, it will be easier to fix your gaze on your goals and to assess whether a particular relationship is in keeping with those goals.

Are you seeking a short-term only dating relationship? If so, be sure anyone you date understands this. Identify your personal guidelines and limits on such a dating relationship. Ask yourself how you will know when to end the relationship. How will you feel if the other person ends the relationship first?

Are you dating for spite? If anger or resentment toward your former spouse is motivating you to date or marry, some serious healing from divorce still needs to occur. If you want to get married to prove to your former spouse that someone values you, then that is a problem too. Both of these reasons for dating suggest a need for continued healing from divorce. Otherwise, strong feelings about your former spouse will stand in the way of a healthy new relationship.

Are you seeking a dating partner to fill a hole that results from not having a mate? If so, you are at risk of settling for less than a good relationship. If you do, you'll likely find yourself unhappy in the end. Dating can be fun, but may also be hazardous to the heart.

Are you ready to find a mate? Before dating, it can be helpful to consider the factors listed below. Otherwise, the lure of romance once a dating relationship has begun may cloud your judgment.

Recognize the Pitfalls of Dating

Dating can have many pitfalls. This is especially true when you are still healing from divorce. Being aware of the risks can help you to keep your feet on level ground.

Emotional Vulnerabilities

A heart that is still vulnerable from the experience of divorce can find rejections and tensions common to the dating world to be particularly hurtful. Even when you have made significant progress in working through the emotions of your divorce, relationship ghosts may surface occasionally.

Trusting Too Quickly

A strong desire for a relationship can result in giving too much trust before knowing someone well. Tread carefully and allow a sense of trust to grow. Knowing when not to trust is important.

Neediness

Excessive neediness can actually make you poor company. Furthermore, neediness does not always attract people who are healthy for you. For example, someone with a low self-esteem may attract a condescending person. This happens because a person with low self-esteem fits perfectly into the needs of a person who wants to feel superior. This perpetuates the first person's low self-esteem. Neediness also makes it hard to set boundaries.

235

Seeking Meaning through Rescue

In an effort to feel needed, some people become romantically involved with a highly needy person. Attempting to find purpose by trying to rescue a person you are dating, leaves you drained in the end. It also shifts your energies away from recovering from your divorce.

Considerations before Serious Dating

Re-entering dating after having been married is a bit scary for many people. Thinking about yourself and about your expectations prior to dating can help. It is important to know yourself, the type of person you are seeking, and to learn as much as you can about healthy relationships.

Remember Who You Are

Knowing your beliefs, values, and rights can help you stay true to yourself when navigating through dating experiences. Identifying the rights you want to claim in a dating relationship is a part of being clear about who you are. Staying true to your values and beliefs builds your sense of self. If someone fails to respect your rights, consider it a red flag of warning.

Proverbs 23:18 says, "There is surely a future hope for you, and your hope will not be cut off." Jeremiah 29:11 promises that God has a plan for you for a future and a hope. You don't have to lower your standards and settle for an unhealthy relationship.

Know the Type of Person You are Seeking

Write a profile of the ideal mate for you. Keep it handy for easy reference. Consider faith, ethics, financial values, personality traits, communication skills, how that person handles conflicts, as well as anything else that is important to you. Consider factors related to a successful future marriage. Use the ideal mate list you develop to remain focused on your goal.

Learn about Healthy Relationships

Learn what goes into making a healthy relationship. Self-help books on relationships allow you to learn on your own. Individual counseling can help you reflect on personal choices and decisions within a relationship as well as life in general. Effective counseling can help you maximize success and minimize risks.

Handling Rejection When Dating

Rejection may be one of the biggest fears of dating and yet it is a natural part of the process. Rejection associated with divorce can magnify sensitivities. Fear of rejection can result in a temptation to submit to unhealthy compromise.

As strange as it sounds, don't take rejection personally. Not being someone else's match does not make you any less valuable. For example, just because a person prefers a Fuji apple over a Golden Delicious apple does not mean there is anything wrong with the Golden Delicious apple. Screening for a good match is an important part of the dating process. Finding your own good match requires doing some weeding out of your own.

Dating and Communication

Be appropriately open about where you are in your life, and what you expect from a relationship. Such transparency will keep the relationship honest and truthful from your end. It will also allow for assessing the potential in a particular relationship more quickly.

> *Two big tears were floating*
> *down the river of time.*
> *They began to engage in conversation.*
> *Said the first tear, 'I am the tear of the girl who*
> *lost her boyfriend to another girl.'*
> *Don't feel so badly,' consoled the other tear.*
> *'I'm the tear of the girl who got him.'*
>
> <u>Serve Him with Mirth,</u> *Flynn 1960* [6] *Used with permission.*

Making Information and Ideas Work

1. What healing do you need to complete prior to dating?

2. If you are ready to date, what are your goals for dating?

3. What pitfalls represent the greatest risks for you?

4. What healthy adjustments do you need to make to avoid those pitfalls?

5. List five things about yourself (beliefs, values, and rights) that are important to consider when dating.

6. Write a profile of your ideal mate.

7. What are your reflections on dating and rejection?

Talk with God--Ponder this reading and share your thoughts with God. Listen so that the Holy Spirit might fill you with wisdom and peace. What concrete actions do you need to take based on what God is saying to you?

Highlights from Chapter 8
Consider What's Next?

1. As you work for renewal after divorce, periodically stop, assess your progress, and determine what you need to do next.

2. Having a dream is the first step toward living that dream.

3. Shifting focus from your marriage and divorce to your own goals and future helps move you forward.

4. Prayerfully developing goals empowers you to set your course for the future while under the shelter of God's wings.

5. The chances of turning a dream into a goal and achieving it are best when you objectively analyze the dream's goal potential.

6. Being wounded or needy does not make a good foundation for being content within yourself or for a having a successful relationship with another person.

7. By nurturing your own healing before dating, you can minimize the pitfalls of a rebound romance.

8. Identifying relationship ghosts is the first step in being able to minimize their impact.

9. Understanding each other's ghosts can help a couple to be more effective in reducing conflicts that result from relationship ghosts of the past.

10. Assessing trust in a dating relationship is easier and safer once you have sufficiently healed your trust wounds.

11. Learning to be wise about trust is important because trust is essential to having a loving relationship.

12. Knowing who you are and having a clear understanding of your expectations regarding dating will help keep your feet on firmer ground.

13. Knowing the pitfalls of dating after divorce can help you minimize your risks.

14. Before you start dating, write a profile of your ideal mate. Keep it handy for easy reference.

15. Not being someone else's match does not make you any less valuable.

16. Finding your purpose in God is about living a glorious life of spiritual vitality. Don't settle for anything less.

---

*You will go out in joy and
be led forth in peace;
the mountains and hills will burst into
song before you, and all the
trees of the field will clap their hands.*

Isaiah 55:12 NIV

Just the Beginning

*So we have not stopped praying for you since we first
heard about you. We ask God to give you complete
knowledge of his will and to give you spiritual wisdom
and understanding. Then the way you live will always
honor and please the Lord, and your lives will produce
every kind of good fruit. All the while, you will grow as
you learn to know God better and better. We also pray
that you will be strengthened with all his glorious power
so you will have all the endurance and patience you need.
May you be filled with joy, always thanking the Father.
He has enabled you to share in the inheritance that belongs to his people, who live in the light. For he has rescued us from the kingdom of darkness and transferred us
into the Kingdom of his dear Son, who purchased our
freedom and forgave our sins.*

Colossians 1:9-14 NLT

The end of this book is the beginning of your future.
Seek other resources you need to help you complete your
journey. Move along at your own pace, but keep moving
forward. God has a plan for you and it is for a future and for
a hope. Seek spiritual wisdom and understanding and your
life will be fruitful and your purpose will become clear.
With God, there is no end. Live in the light and freedom of
the Holy Spirit as you work through all of life's new begin-
nings. Blessings!

NOTES:

Chapter 2
Page 34
[1]Reinhold Niebuhr, "The Serenity Prayer," (Public domain) as cited on "Inspiration, Learning, and Support for Hearing God's Voice." *The Voice for Love.* http://www.thevoiceforlove.com/serenity-prayer.html (accessed July 16, 2010).

Chapter 4
Page 114
[2]------"Laughter Helps Blood Vessels Function Better," March 7, 2005. http://www.umm.edu/news/releases/laughter2.htm (accessed February 10, 2010).

Chapter 5
Page 140
[3]Roberta Grace, "Steps to Total Forgiveness," unpublished material, Charleston, South Carolina, 2008.

Chapter 7
Page 193
[4]Mary Elizabeth Hughes and Linda J. Waite, "Marital Biography and Health at Mid-Life," 2009.
http://hsb.sagepub.com/cgi/content/abstract/50/3/344 (accessed March 15, 2010).

Page 194
[5]Don Colbert, *What You Don't Know May Be Killing You.* Lake Mary, FLA: Siloam, A Strang Company, 2004, p 89.

Chapter 8
Page 238
[6]Flynn, "Serve Him with Mirth," p. 61 as cited on "Internet Evangelism Day. 1960. http://www.internetevangelismday.com/mirth.php (accessed July 15, 2010.)

Bibliography

------. *Laughter Helps Blood Vessels Function Better.* March 7, 2005. http://www.umm.edu/news/releases/laughter2.htm (accessed February 10, 2010).

Brooks, Robert, and Sam Goldstein. *The Power of Resilience.* New York, NY: The McGraw Hill Companies, 2004.

Cloud, Henry, and John Townsend. *Boundaries -- When to Say Yes, When to Say No to take Control of Your Life.* Grand Rapids, MI: Zondervan, 1992.

Colbert, Don. *What You Don't Know May Be Killing You.* Lake Mary, FLA: Siloam, A Strang Company, 2004.

Fisher, Bruce, and Robert Alberti. *Rebuilding When Your Relationship Ends.* Atascadero, CA: Impact Publishers, Inc., 2006.

Flynn, Leslie. "Serve Him with Mirth (p. 61)." *Internet Evangelism Day.* 1960. http://www.internetevangelismday.com/mirth.php (accessed July 15, 2010).

Friedman, Russell, and John James. "The Myth of the Stages of Dying, Death and Grief." *The Grief Recovery Institute Web site.* 2008. http://www.grief.net/Articles/Myth%20of%20Stages.pdf (accessed 2009).

Grace, Roberta. "Steps to Total Forgiveness, unpublished material." Charleston, South Carolina, 2008.

Grudem, Wayne. *Systematic Theology.* Grand Rapids, MI: Inter-Varsity Press, Zondervan Publishing House, 1994.

Hughes, Mary Elizabeth, and Linda J. Waite. *Marital Biography and Health at Mid-Life.* 2009. http://hsb.sagepub.com/cgi/content/abstract/50/3/344 (accessed March 15, 2010).

James, John W., and Russell Friedman. *The Grief Recovery Handbook.* New York, NY: HaperCollins, 1998.

Niebuhr, Reinhold. "Inspiration, Learning, and Support for Hearing God's Voice." *The Voice for Love.* http://www.thevoiceforlove.com/serenity-prayer.html (accessed July 16, 2010).

Index

245

Learn how to start a
Peace after Divorce Workshop
Group Ministry at Your Church

Visit www.afterdivorceministries.com

Insights from a Past Participant:

To me, divorce was like a hurricane, everything in my life was in turmoil and uncertainty. This ministry put me in the eye of the storm, where I had the opportunity calmly to gather among new friends and gradually to take on directions for my life. From feeling like a storm victim, I became a beloved child of God on the way to a victorious future.

Charles Howard

You may contact Renee Ettline by emailing her at info@afterdivorceministries.com.

246

Made in the USA
Columbia, SC
28 September 2020